Copyright @ Jennifer Ellen Hamer 2021

All rights reserved. No part of this publication may be reproduced, stored in a retrieval system or transmitted in any form, electronic, mechanical, photocopying or recording without permission in writing from the publisher.

Jennifer Ellen Hamer is to be identified as the author of this work.

Cover design

Abigail Gatling, Crisp Communications Co

Editors

Karly Bartrim
Frazer Pearce

Mission Statement

I aim to bring hope, inspiration, and support to all those suffering with eating disorders. I hope I can help make treatment accessible for every single person affected by an eating disorder. I want to break down the stigma attached to these deadly illnesses and to help society have a greater understanding of eating disorders. I will dedicate the rest of my life to help save lives and be an advocate for eating disorders.

Dedicated to every single person affected by an eating disorder. Never give up hope.

I want to thank every single person who has played their part in my recovery journey, but especially my loving family, Mum, Dad and Jo, who held my hand and continue to do so every step of the way.

Thank you to Scott Heathwood who introduced me to the incredible Abigail Gatling who not only produced the most beautiful book cover, but also played a huge role in ensuring this project of mine came together as planned.

Lastly, to the Gold Coast Open Water Swimming Club, who since moving to Australia have without realising helped to keep me pushing forward on my path. As we say, "just keep swimming".

Contents

Preface - Goodbye Anna	4
Childhood joys	6
The big change	9
The battles begin	14
A glimpse of Jen	24
Sporting dreams	28
Back on the slippery slope	31
Taken to rock bottom	34
Life as an inpatient	39
The day my freedom was taken away	47
Cheesecake and cream	57
A fragile diagnosis	64
Complex chronic pain	69
The day of freedom	72
A family holiday minus Anna	76
University goals	80
A beautiful friendship	85
Questions in recovery	89
Christmas 2018	95
New chapters in Australia	112
Sweet tastes of life	118
Ocean swimming, roadblocks and baby news	125
Family reunion, Charlie's Christmas 2021	127
A pause, for now!	130
To the reader who may be supporting a loved one	135
Farewell!	138

Preface – Goodbye Anna

Thank you for choosing to pick up this book and for making your way to the first page of the most honest story I will ever share. This book was a promise that I made to myself the day I chose to commit to recovery; I vowed that one day I would be brave enough and well enough to share my story with the world.

My aim in this book is to recount my 16-year journey with anorexia. Not to seek sympathy or approval, but hopefully to inspire others who may be trapped under the rules of anorexia or working on their own journey of recovery. I also hope this book can provide insight for those who may not understand so much about eating disorders. To let you inside of the mind of someone with that lived experience, to help you understand the complexities of these illnesses and break down the stigma attached to eating disorders. I will share my harrowing journey and demonstrate that recovery is always an option. I almost lost my life to anorexia. I was told I would die, but I defied the odds. My recovery journey is ongoing however I want to dedicate my future to being a voice of hope, courage and bravery in eating disorder recovery, to serve as a mental health campaigner and to help prevent others from having to go through the same thing.

I want to help save lives.

The book will take you from my early childhood days when life was truly amazing, before diving into the darkest of patches, when anorexia took hold. We will also experience some of the brighter moments when I started to regain life again and venture on the journey of recovery. The truth is it is rather messy; recovery is never linear. There are many bumps in the road, but I hope you can follow my tale.

Interspersed throughout my journey, you will stumble across letters I have written to family and also Anna (anorexia) herself. If you are in the early phases of recovery, I would advise you to wait before reading this book, as there may be a few triggers if you are not yet in the full recovery mindset.

Writing this book was a challenge, reliving some of my darkest days, bringing up some of those overwhelming emotions that consumed me for so many years, but at the same time, it has enabled me to appreciate the journey I have been on, to be proud of where I have come from and excited about where I will go next. I hope my story will provide you with hope, inspire you if that is what you need right now. Or, if you're someone who wants to learn more, I hope it will help you begin to understand how an eating disorder literally takes someone's life away. How recovery can help reclaim that life and know that you – yes, you reading this can be a fundamental part of someone's recovery journey.

This is my story. It's a story of courage, strength, and determination. One where I found courage and chose to fight. Fight to save myself, to not only reclaim a life I deserved, but I would be able to help save others.

It goes a little like this…

Childhood joys

I was born on 1st October 1991 in Kent to a loving family. I had two incredible parents to nurture me and a wonderful older sister to look up to. My sister, Jo, was 3 years older than me, born on the 28th of September 1988. Growing up, Jo and I spent so much time playing together, having fun, laughing and just being mischievous little girls. We were very happy children.

Happiness is a word that I think gets thrown around all too much without truly understanding what it means. As a child, I don't even think I ever considered what this word meant, but I can tell you one thing, I knew I was full of happiness. In fact, I think I fitted the very definition of the word. My childhood years were the best. As I sit here writing this, I feel so incredibly grateful for the fact I was brought into this world by a wonderful family, who would love and support me as I grew. How they would provide me with all I needed to be healthy and happy, how blessed I was.

Like most young children, I loved playing with my toys, I loved being outside, especially in the garden playing any game that resembled some form of sport. From the age of two, I had mastered the idea that a bat was used to hit a ball, the pedals turned the bike wheels, and my legs would move fast to run. I was a child with no fear, who had a cheeky streak, always trying to push the boundaries, but never too far, as I hated being in trouble. Looking back, my primary school years were also some of my favourite times. I was happy and precocious; I excelled at sport but didn't like art. I was good at math's and science but lagged behind in English. I was sassy and adventurous, but also a little stubborn and I was known for sulking if I didn't get my way (not much has changed to this day there!). From an early age, I thrived on praise and loved to win. I looked up to my big sister Jo, who always held my hand, guided me forward and showed me the way. I had lots of friends to play with, I was popular. I loved my family dearly – my favourite times were holidays in Portugal and big family Christmases when we would play the craziest of games. I was a competitive little girl who always pushed and pushed to make sure she won her races, always striving to be the best.

I can't really complain about anything in my childhood. Without sounding too confident in myself, I was successful at most things; excelling in school and winning sports matches. I would be praised for my achievements, and from the tender age of six, I realised I thrived off external validation. Providing I was receiving this, I knew that I felt good enough. I felt the "best", and that's all I wanted to be. But even from this young age, it was apparent I was a sensitive child. When I was sad, I would try to hide my emotions and just get on with life. I didn't share how I was feeling very often.

Sport was always a prominent feature during my youth and continues to be today. I loved all sports. My family would say I was a little tomboy. Every day when I got home from school, I would play outside with my friends who lived next door until Mum called me in to get ready to go to an evening sports club, whether that was athletics, netball, cricket, swimming, or tennis. I got involved in whatever I could. However, the two sports where I excelled most were running and cricket. I was very competitive, maybe a little too competitive sometimes. I wanted to be an athlete of some sort and looking back it saddens me to know I was not able to pursue this dream I wished for.

My relationship with food was like most children. I ate what I was given and didn't really spend much energy or time thinking about it, apart from the fact I either liked the taste of something or not. My favourite meals included salmon with rice and peas, topped with tomato ketchup (no judgement please), Nan's chicken pie with boiled potatoes, carrots and broccoli, or I loved a Chinese take way (especially carefully constructing the duck pancakes and all the components that went inside). I enjoyed most things, and I wasn't fussy. Like most children, I responded to my hunger cues, asking for food when I was hungry and stopping eating when I was full. Mum fed my sister and me well, and we grew up loving food, all foods.

Summing my childhood up; I got to experience the wild, innocent and ignorant freedom of life.

The big change

Having been an A grade student, I moved from my village community primary school to a large Grammar School at the age of 11. I was excited; I was going to join my sister at a very well-respected school. I was a confident girl which comforted my family in believing that I would be fine with the transition.

The first day of secondary school arrived and I remember walking into what was a highly competitive environment. A large, all-girls' grammar school. How does a perfectionist prepare herself to leave a nurturing village primary where she's been the centre of attention for the past six years, to enter a large, all-girls' school where suddenly she feels she is just one of the crowd?

I instantly felt lost.

I started comparing myself to other girls, many of whom were smaller than me. I was by no means big, but I was tall for my age and a little more developed. I didn't like this. I wanted to be small like them, I wanted to stay a child, I didn't want to change. I believed they were prettier than me too. I felt I wasn't good enough anymore and I didn't know how to manage the emotions that came with feeling that way.

Each day, I would find myself comparing to others. Thinking that they were more intelligent than me, faster than me at running, or more popular than me. This was the first time I had ever felt I wanted to be someone other than myself. I didn't love 'me' anymore. As time passed, this hatred towards myself became worse, and I would lose concentration in lessons because my mind wouldn't stop with these thoughts of wanting to be someone else. I didn't know at the time this was the start of a long battle I would face with my own mind.

It was break time at school. My friends and I were in the canteen, sitting down quietly like all the other first graders, respecting the rules. The older students did anything and everything they could to push their luck with the canteen staff. I had my own snack with me. A Nutrigrain bar – a breakfast-type bar with a soft wholegrain outer layer and a yummy fruit purée filling (my favourite was the blueberry flavour). I opened the wrapper and started to eat, without even really paying much attention to the food, apart from the fact I liked the taste of these snack bars. Quite the normal response of a child eating what she had been given by her mum. However, one of my friends picked up the wrapper and started scanning the back.

"What are you looking at?" I asked her, unsure what she was doing.

"Oh, I'm reading how many calories are in this bar," she replied.

"What are calories?" I asked, looking puzzled.

She also looked puzzled at my remark, confused that I didn't know what a calorie was. She responded with a full explanation for me.

"Well, they are like units of energy. You are meant to eat so many of them each day. If you eat too many, you'll gain weight! Healthy foods like fruits and vegetables have less calories, and unhealthy foods like chocolate and sweets have more."

It was that moment my blindness to diet culture was shattered. I was a young girl who loved the body she lived in; it felt like a good place to live. I had grown up without any awareness that 'diet culture' even existed. I'd been a little girl who enjoyed all foods for what they were, who had

a healthy relationship with food and was taught it is never about what is on the outside, but what is on the inside that counts. But that was not what the outside world was telling me. I had just been exposed to the toxic industry that is diet culture, a culture that values weight, shape and size over health and wellbeing.
This was the precise point when something changed for me. It was as if my mind joined a few dots together. Recognising I no longer felt the "best" at math, or sport, or anything else for that matter, I questioned if I could become the best at monitoring my calorie intake. I decided I would only eat those 'healthy foods,' and it will provide me with that sense of being perfect again. It all started quite innocently. I decided I would stop eating chocolate for a while. I also decided to stop eating sweets. I went home from school that day and told Mum of my plans. She wasn't alarmed at first, just listened with care as she always did. I seem to remember her suggesting that I didn't need to cut out these foods completely, maybe just have them a little less often, but that wasn't good enough for me. If I was going to do this, it had to be perfect.

So, I started replacing chocolate and sweets with fruits, deemed as me trying to be 'healthy'. But even in these early stages, looking back, I can see how this new plan of mine had already started compromising my happy childhood memories. One of which was our weekly Sunday morning outing with my grandad. We would walk together, gramps, my sister and I to the village river to feed the ducks, and on the way, we'd stop at the penny sweet shop, where he would let us have a bag of pick 'n' mix sweets each. This was such a treat. I loved our Sunday mornings with Grandad. Jo always picked the fizzy belts and red liquorice straws; I was more into the foam bananas and strawberry laces and the Percy Pigs. But now I'd stopped eating sweets, this Sunday morning ritual changed. Whilst Jo would pick her sweets and enjoy the tastes and textures of these yummy treats, I waited, refusing to let down on the rules I had created. I could sense Grandad's sadness when he offered to buy us our usual sweets, and I said I didn't want any… I went without.

The elimination of chocolate and sweets lasted a couple of weeks, but the novelty soon wore off. I didn't get the same sense of achievement and control that I'd initially felt. I'd also realised that other people were successfully cutting out chocolate and sweets too. I was no longer the best at this. I decided I would need to do more. I thought about what I could try next to strive for perfection with my food intake. Not knowing much about nutrition at this tender age, I decided I would Google *'healthy foods'* and *'low-calorie foods'*. This provided me with a wealth of information…

I was soon exposed to the toxic place the internet can be, filled with diet culture flooding my brain. Google taught me too much of what I didn't need to know. I soon became an expert of knowing the calories of pretty much every food. I read up on what foods I could cut out next, and over the next few weeks I continued to cut back on other foods deemed 'unhealthy'. With this I got that sense of empowerment and strength. I was fulfilling my need to feel like I was the best at something again. I became completely obsessed. I remember at school I had to make sure as soon as the lunch bell went, I ran to the canteen to buy a small salad to eat before my sister got there because I didn't want her to see. I needed to hide my secrets from her. My thoughts became consumed and dominated by food, calories, and exercise. My self-restraint became quite phenomenal, but this does not surprise me. I had always been determined, dedicated and ambitious with anything I ever did.

As time went on my family became more concerned. Dad didn't say anything to me, but I knew he was worried. Mum raised the conversation one evening about whether I was ok. She gently suggested I relaxed the rules I had created and try to be a little kinder to myself. She reminded me that all the foods I'd cut out weren't bad for me when eaten in moderation, and they were all foods I had loved before my decisions to eliminate them. But I was stubborn and determined to stick to my plans. I refused her advice and explained that I felt much happier eating this way. But was I? This is where I share with you the first encounter with anorexia or Anna as I named it.

Anna was the voice of anorexia in my head. I describe it as sharing my brain with someone else. It wasn't really me. Little did I know Anna would slowly begin to take complete control over me.

The battles begin

As time went on my weight began to drop and my family became more concerned. My sister had spotted me buying small pots of salad at lunch and nothing else. She knew something was wrong. While I loved vegetables, I was never a big fan of salad as a child and all of a sudden it was the foundations of every meal I ate. I was lethargic and had little energy to do sports or schoolwork. I did not want to acknowledge that this had anything to do with the fact that I was starving my body.

Mum suggested we go to the doctor and see if he could help. It was pretty obvious why I was tired all the time, but as I was trying to ignore this reality, I agreed to go along. Mum and I went to the surgery together and I explained to the GP that I was feeling tired a lot and lacked energy. He asked about my eating patterns and I said I was eating plenty and trying to eat healthily.

"She has cut out certain foods such as chocolate, cakes, crisps, biscuits and other foods she once loved," Mum said.

I remember shooting her a look of pure rage, which was so unlike me. I quickly jumped in to make sure the doctor didn't take Mum's side. I needed him on mine.

"Yes, I'm just trying to eat foods that are better for my health at the moment. I enjoy eating healthily."

The doctor supported my word, as I gave an inward sigh of relief. He simply encouraged me to maybe consume more of the foods I felt comfortable with such as fruit and vegetables. He also said he'd run some blood tests to make sure everything was OK. On leaving, I was discreetly happy with the outcome, while Mum seemed disappointed but didn't make a fuss, after all he was the healthcare professional. I think that at this stage she didn't want to believe I had an eating disorder, but I think she already knew deep down what was going on. She had first-hand experience, having had her own battle with anorexia when she was much younger. The last thing she wanted was for her daughter to suffer in the same way.

A week later, we got the blood test results from the doctor, which suggested I had a case of glandular fever. The doctor explained that this was probably why I felt like I had very little energy and lacked appetite. My family and I knew this was not the only reason I had little energy, but because of the diagnosis they just accepted it for the time being. I was told by the doctor I would need to take some days off school and spend time resting at home. I was fine to miss school, although I felt little concerned at how I could avoid eating if I was at home in the presence of Mum who would also be there. Also, hearing the word rest did not sit well with me, or Anna at least. I chose to completely ignore the face he told me to rest. By this stage, it was quite clear I had become brainwashed by Anna. I was obsessed with food and exercise. Sport no longer provided me with the joy it once did. It was something I had to do, a chore, whether I was tired or not. Anna was in complete control of me, she was my dictator and I obeyed everything she told me. I started isolating myself from everyone, declining invites from friends to go out, instead choosing to hide in my bedroom and finding ways to exercise at every spare moment I had.

Weeks went by and instead of getting better from *'glandular fever'* by *'resting'* at home, I was getting weaker as I continued to cut more foods out of my diet and cut back on portion sizes. I was becoming sneaky at mealtimes too. If Mum served me something that Anna didn't approve of, I would scoop it into a napkin and when no one was watching place it on my lap and dispose of it after. Sometimes this was harder than others, but I was becoming better and better at learning how to deceive my family.

When I returned to school after my time off, I remember my friends being so friendly and kind, yet I had little enthusiasm for engaging in their conversation. I also spent some time working out ways that I could continue to adhere to Anna's rules while at school. I soon came up with a plan that involved running to the canteen at lunchtime to buy some salad, eat it quickly before my friends arrived and then spend the remainder of lunch pacing aimlessly around school, my skeletal frame resisting the urge to stop until the bell went for the end of lunch. I would also do this during morning break time to burn off as much food that passed my lips as possible. I remember people staring at me, puzzled at this lifeless soul on her own, everyday walking and walking around the school campus, whilst they were doing all the fun normal things teenagers do, laughing, playing silly games, and getting up to mischief.

At the end of the day, I would get the school bus home. As soon as it arrived back in my home village, I would step off before racing home, leaving my sister to walk on her own. I would rush through the door after quickly greeting mum so I could get to my bedroom and engage in brutal exercise regimes; press ups, star jumps, sit ups, sprinting on the spot (all the while trying not to make too much noise and risk being heard). Only after completing this military regime would I allow myself the small portion of dinner Mum cooked.

After dinner, I would run straight back up to my bedroom and repeat the same exercise regime. I couldn't bear the thought of food being inside of me. Anna had made me believe that if I exercised straight after meals, I would burn off anything I had just eaten; she distorted my intelligence and made me believe the most irrational things. Before bed, I would recall everything I ate that day, even though it would be the same day in day out. But I needed to do this to comfort me, ensuring I hadn't consumed more than I was 'allowed'. It also was a way for me to feel in control. I felt like I had succeeded if I recalled everything that I did, which adhered to Anna's rules. If Mum had tried to get me to eat something different (which I would have refused anyway), I would google how many calories were in it. I would sit there feeling convinced she was just trying to make me fat.

I was becoming weaker and weaker, but Anna was thriving, gaining strength all the time. In a paradoxical way, despite the pain she was causing me I felt Anna was becoming my best friend, my only friend. I was excited to have a friend who was with me every moment of the day. Anna was always with me, and despite my body being weak, she provided me with this sense of strength, satisfaction, and control. For all the times I felt unsafe, obeying the rules of Anna meant I felt like I had some sort of control and created a blanket of safety around me. I was becoming the best at adhering to the rules she set. Anna understood me and I understood her. Anna commended me when I followed her orders, and that was what I thrived off, receiving validation. Up to then, I had lived with very little self-worth, but Anna made me feel valued. She made me feel that maybe I was good enough for this world, providing I obeyed her rules. But I knew that to make sure this relationship lasted; I would have to make sure I followed these rules religiously and continuously. There would be no breaking them, or else Anna our partnership would fail, I would fail.

Family arguments became a regular occurrence. I had lost my relationship I had with my sister and I continued each day to push her away. It was so sad. Growing up, we shared such a special bond yet Anna destroyed that. This was how I behaved towards anyone who tried to care and support me. I would push them away, detaching myself from any emotions or social connection. I was a cold individual, seemingly rude and blank in expression. Food and exercise helped me to manage emotions I didn't want to feel, and these tools became my coping mechanisms.

Anna was brilliant at helping me to numb emotions, whether these were joyful or painful. I couldn't feel when someone was trying to care for me. I couldn't tell when I was hurtful to others. Turning to food and exercise were the only things I could focus on, a focus that I felt was providing me with direction, purpose, and achievement. At this time, Anna was the only one I wanted to be close to, the only one supporting my behaviour. The only one who helped me avoid the emotions I did not want to explore, yet ironically the very ones I needed to feel to express myself.

I became an absolute nightmare to live with. I was becoming a spiteful, malicious and self-centred girl, preoccupied with food and exercise. Quite the opposite to the qualities I had growing up. I did all I had to do to adhere to Anna's rules, to please her. I did not care what lengths I went to achieve this, and it breaks my heart to say this, but it occasionally involved physical fighting with loved ones. I was horrible to be around when under the dictatorship of Anna. But I couldn't let Anna down. We were a team. I had devoted all of me to Anna, I trusted her and she was the only one now who mattered.

I was falling deeper into anorexia day by day. My family were becoming increasingly worried for my health and decided it was time to take me back to the doctor. Mum and I returned to the GP, and this time it wasn't so easy for me to convince him I was fine. As we entered his consulting room, Mum spoke before the doctor could even say anything.

"I believe Jennifer has anorexia, and she needs help."

Just as before, I darted Mum a look of rage and anger for her words.

"No, I don't!" I snapped back quickly. *"I'm just trying to live healthily, that's all."*

The doctor peered at me and said he wanted to weigh me.

After putting me on the scales and listening to mum express her concern over my behaviors and watching her daughter disappear before her eyes, he said he understood her concerns and also believed I needed some help. He suggested we attend an appointment at a specialist clinic to get an assessment. He made it clear that if they agreed with me and didn't think I had an eating disorder, we would consider an alternative diagnosis.

I reluctantly agreed to go, but I was sure that somehow I could muster up a plan to convince them I didn't have an eating disorder. I spent the whole of the next day consumed with what I was going to say; how I was going to navigate this? I look back and question how someone as sick as I was believed she could convince a medical team specializing in eating disorders that she was fine. I also find it terrifying that the doctor would only refer me to treatment once I met a weight criteria. This highlighting how eating disorders are still so misunderstood even by the medical world. Eating disorders are mental illnesses with the highest mortality rate of any psychiatric illness. To have a mental illness, you can be any weight, shape, or size. Yet to be diagnosed with anorexia, medics continue to focus on appearance as a diagnostic, which is wrong and explains why so many people are refused help.

Mum, Dad and I went along to the appointment together. We were greeted by an older lady with a stern look on her face.

"Jennifer, can you explain to me what has been going on? How are you feeling?" She asked me.

"I've just been trying to eat healthily and exercise regularly to look after myself," I replied.

Without allowing me to speak further, she interrupted.

"You have not been eating healthily according to my report here. There is no question in my mind that you have

anorexia, and from my experience if you do not choose to get better you will end up in hospital."
She turned to my Mum and dad.

"You must take control over Jennifer's eating and exercise habits. Otherwise, she will end up being admitted to an inpatient unit, and that is not what any of you want to happen."

I remember feeling so much loathing for this lady. She was ruining everything, so blunt, to the point and showed no empathy.

"I am not listening to anything you say. You don't know me, you don't understand me, and I don't have anorexia," I shouted.

Tears were streaming by now – not just down my face, but my parents too. I stormed out of the room, only to be dragged back in.

"Jennifer, if you do not comply with receiving treatment, there will be no alternative but to go into hospital, and I can arrange that now," she explained.

Mum turned to me and put her hand on mine.

"Darling, listen to the doctor. She is trying to help you. Please, Jennifer, we can do this together," pleaded mum.

I whipped my hand away and didn't respond. This was exactly what Anna didn't want to happen.

"I shall book Jennifer an appointment with the dietician tomorrow, who will work on a meal plan. You must ensure that Jennifer adheres to it. You will need to join her at lunchtime at school everyday to make sure she eats her lunch and watch her at every mealtime," the doctor instructed.

We left the appointment. I was not speaking to my parents and refused to even look at them. We drove home in complete silence, tension building between us. When we arrived home, I ignored my sister as she welcomed me through the front door. I ran to my room and lay on my bed crying.

Later that night Mum, came in and tried to comfort me.

"Jennifer, darling, I know you are angry. I know you hate us right now, but we love you so much, and we just want to help you. We want to see you play the sport like you used to. We want you to be happy."

I refused to engage in any discussion or acknowledge the love and support my family were giving me. I was nothing but rude and unresponsive. Eventually, Mum gave up. She cried as she left the room but turned back for a moment.

"I love you, Jen. I always will, even if you don't love me."

But it wasn't me, it was Anna! Jen loved her family dearly, but I just couldn't find myself beneath the terrible power of Anna. She had me in her control. The next day we went to my first dietitian appointment, and I was given a meal plan that horrified me. It involved so much food compared to what I was eating. I spent the entire appointment trying to work out ways to avoid consuming things or eliminate foods, without anyone realizing. With Anna in control, I had so many tricks up my sleeve and felt confident I could get rid of most foods I didn't want to eat. There were many ways I could still exercise, so that would ensure I was ridding myself of those calories. However, Mum was even more determined to keep a watchful eye on me from now on. This was evident that night when she came to my room with a glass of strawberry milk, which was on the meal plan. She said I had to drink it. I refused and said I wouldn't. Her response was not what I was expecting. Mum had listened to the doctor and decided she needed to be cruel to be kind.

"Jennifer, I am not leaving this room until you drink the milk, and I don't mind how long this takes."

I sat there thinking that she would give in at some stage. She wouldn't sit there for that long. But Mum was not leaving. I began to cry and bury my head in my pillow. It was late, I was tired. Mum was also tired, but she was not giving in. I just wanted to sleep, escape all of this and get out of my own head.

"I just wish she would go away," I muttered quietly.

"Who, darling?"

"This voice in my head that's telling me everything I can and cannot eat. She is controlling everything I do, and I want her to go away."

Mum pulled me up into her arms and gave me the biggest cuddle. *"Jen, together we'll get her to leave you alone,"* she assured me.

"But please, you must try to drink this milk. How about I go and get a glass for myself too, and we drink it together?"

I looked at her with the tiniest glimpse of trust and hope and nodded. Mum came back with her own glass of strawberry milk. After many more battles with myself (and a few more tears), I eventually managed to find the courage and strength to drink the milk, slowly. Sip by sip we did it together. I felt disgusted with myself after. I felt like I had betrayed Anna. She was shouting at me. Yet, Mum was praising me and hugging me so tight. I was so confused, riddled with anxiety and felt completely lost in myself. We hugged before she left me late in the night, falling into a deep sleep.

The next day it was as if a huge weight had been lifted. It may have been a very small step, but the previous night was the first time in a long time that Mum had seen a glimmer of Jen and not Anna. It was the first time I'd acknowledged I wanted help. I wanted this voice to stop controlling my life – and that in itself was huge because this acknowledgement meant there was a route for my family to support me on this journey. It wasn't going to be easy, but together we could overcome this.

Moving forward my life consisted of endless appointments; counsellors trying to help me and a dietitian also there providing my meal plans and weighing me at every appointment. We tried family therapy, but this would frequently end in arguments as Anna fought back. My mind was in constant battles with glimmers of hope wanting to recover. However Anna continued to remind me, she was the only one I could trust, the only one who understood me. My own mind was exhausting me each day and night. It never stopped.

Mum would leave her job at lunchtime each day. She'd take me out of school to a park, where together we'd sit and eat my packed lunch, and she would make sure I was eating all of it. She knew how hard this was for me. I trembled with every bite, but at the same time there was a very small part of me that was happy; happy that I was giving myself permission to eat foods I'd once loved, foods that tasted good. It was often after a meal that my anxiety would increase, and I'd feel such disgust towards myself and my body. But I had to deal with those emotions because there was no going back. Slowly, we started to make progress. I saw we because this was not a battle I was facing on my own, this was very much a team effort from my family, care team and me. I was eating regularly, sticking to the meal plan, and gaining weight. However, eating disorders are sneaky and will do anything to hold on to you, to keep you gripped in any way possible. I had to eat everything I was given, so anorexia kept hold of me through ensuring I complied to a brutal daily exercise regime. I was exercising every moment I could find, in my bedroom, at school, multiple daily walks… whenever, wherever I could.

A glimpse of Jen

I was about to reach my 14th birthday and I had been making good progress with my recovery. I was managing to eat a wider variety of foods again and adhere to a regular eating pattern with meals and snacks. I was even finding joy and contentment with some of the foods I was eating. Despite my progress, I still maintained very regimented and controlled eating patterns and rules about what I could have and when I could have it. I would not deviate from my meal plan. If I was asked to try something new, I would be overwhelmed with anxiety and struggle to overcome these fears. It was such a gripping control element I held on to in attempt to feel "safe".

I continued to have issues with certain foods, which were the foods I had cut out in the first stages of my eating disorder: chocolate, sweets, fried foods, and anything Anna still deemed unhealthy. If I did so happen to challenge these behaviors, Anna would remind me I would fail if I disobeyed her any more than I was already doing so. Consequently, I would return to the 'new' rules I had created around what I could and couldn't eat. It was my way of feeling safe, my comfort zone, a place where I could feel in control. I felt like I had no other choice. I had to prove to Anna I was good enough.

Looking back, I can see how I was still governed by Anna's rules at this time. When we would go for dinner as a family, which was once such a special treat that I would look forward too. Now I would always have to pick the restaurant in advance ensuring that they served food that would fit with my rules so that we didn't arrive, and I would have a anxiety episode refusing to eat. Even when we did arrive at the restaurant, I would often still request changes to the meal when ordering. This filtered into many other occasions in life. I would have to take food with me to events and gatherings as I would not feel ok about eating less familiar foods. I could not be spontaneous like other girls my age. For most teenage girls going to events and parties was an exciting occasion to socialize, create memories. Yet for me, my mind was consumed about the food that would be available. While people at these events never used to say anything or question me on my strange behaviors. They were very aware something wasn't quite right, and I guess that just learnt to accept me as "that girl with an eating disorder". Strangely I think some part of me almost thrived off this, and maybe it comes back to always feeling like I needed attention to find something inside that confirmed my worth in this world.

Despite these challenges I continued to experience each day, my family were beginning to see a glimpse of Jen again. Occasionally that would catch me laughing and smiling. I had a sense that I was starting to step towards life once more. I was happy to spend time with my friends and was slowly making a return to sport – something I had missed so much. Although I would be lying to say my relationship with exercise was healthy.

My relationship with sport had changed. There was part of me that still loved my sport for what it was; I had always enjoyed sport, and I was a talented athlete. I loved how it made me feel, I loved being competitive, and I loved the excitement and thrill it provided me with. I loved nothing more than challenging my body, moving and being active. Before anorexia, I did not associate exercise with burning off calories or changing my physique. I participated for pure enjoyment and to express my competitive spirit. However, once Anna came into my life, sporting activities were now governed by my obsession with exercise and burning calories. These two relationships seemed to merge together. I still had this immense passion for sport, but at the same time, I was frequently reminded that I was adhering to Anna's rules for exercise. It was so sad. She was destroying the healthy relationship I had developed with sport and exercise growing up and to this day I still struggle to regain that innocence of being able to immerse myself in exercise without the pure purpose of experiencing moving my body in a way that feels invigorating.

Nevertheless, despite these challenges with my relationship with exercise, I was starting to have some great success with my sport, and this made me so happy. I was feeling like an athlete again! I was back running for my local athletics club, where I was regularly selected to represent the county. I was getting faster, winning races, and feeling like I was back on track. I was opening the batting for the county cricket team, being able to once again find that competitive little Jen that had been trapped inside for so long. The more I got back to my sport, the more success I began to have. However, I was always still slightly on the back foot. I wasn't quite the best that I knew I could be. I often wonder what I could have achieved if I was living in a healthy body without an eating disorder? While I was functionally performing, and seen as a young athlete with 'real potential', I was also in a body that had never had a menstrual cycle, always carrying an injury and permanently under fueling for the activity I was participating in.

I would describe myself at this time as functionally recovered. I was obsessed with exercise, and I was terrified of certain foods. I could no longer pour a "non-measured" bowl of cereal to drown in milk. I could no longer get excited when choosing a birthday cake. I was unable to savor the sweet icing until last. Memories of buying yummy sweets from the sweet shop with my Grandad seemed to be fast fading. And ordering what I truly wanted off the menu instead of the healthy option was a memory of the past. I could no longer enjoy my favorite dessert of apple crumble and warm custard or see food to be all about the taste and not about numbers. Christmas dinner was no longer a selection of yummy foods. Instead, it was a list of ingredients that diet culture made me fearful of.

Despite the loss of all these joyful experiences I could no longer partake in, I was able to function through life in a society that has somewhat normalised these behaviors.

Sporting dreams

Aged 17 and I was reaching the point with my sport where I was excelling, especially with my athletics potential. I was having great success with my commitment to long distance running and genuinely believed I could become an elite runner. It became a bit of a dream to aim to get a Great Britain vest under my belt and gain a title of running for England. I believed I could.

This desire to become an elite runner soon became my identity, and I became known in my home village as the *'runner girl'*. I was getting up at 5am to head out for my morning run before school and then after school, I had training at the athletics track with the squad. It was intense and I am still surprised that I could commit to this amount of training, considering that I was still engaging in such disordered eating behaviors, and yet to have a menstrual cycle. But I continued to suppress all my struggles, I had one goal and I was determined to try to achieve it. I didn't even contemplate the damage I was doing to my body, training to this level without a menstrual cycle, without nourishing my body.

While I adored running and connected to it on so many levels, again the relationship I had developed with exercise meant I did use it as a way to control my physique, to manage my eating disorder and it turned in to another means of control. The rigid, demanding and regimented training regimes fitted nicely with Anna's rules.

As I approached the end of my school education, with my A level results pending, it was almost time to move on to university. I struggled during the last two years of education, as I had moved secondary schools, which was a significant change in my life. I started at a new school at

the age of 17 without any friends and had to start from scratch. Anna joined me on this new venture, which meant I already had barriers in place to prevent me from making new friends. I had to stick to Anna's rules so when any opportunities did arise for me to socialize with others, offering an opportunity to make friends I would decline. This would normally be at lunch time; I would turn down the kind offer to join others for lunch, instead choosing to go for a long and aimless walk on my own to burn off calories. These two years doing final exams at school were lonely years. I isolated myself completely, made no friends and was a complete outcast. Nevertheless, somehow, I managed to get through my exams and achieve the results I needed to get into university. I had received an offer from both universities I had applied for. First, St Mary's, a small university that had a great sporting and academic reputation.
Second, Brunel University, a very large university which was also renowned for their incredible success in producing internationally competing athletes.

I remember visiting the universities with dad. He was there to support me but reminded me that this was my decision. He could advise me but could not make the decision for me. I knew however that Dad felt I would be best at St Mary's. I had always excelled in smaller environments. Maybe, this was because I learnt from a young age in my small and safe primary school how to thrive in small and contained environments. Yet I was attracted to Brunel, it had everything I wanted. The training facilities were incredible, and they were consistently producing world-class athletes. I judged a book by its cover it you like, and I decided I would accept my place at Brunel where I would study for a sports science degree.

September soon came around. It was the first time I would leave my little village, living with my family to live on my own at university to study for my degree and aim to pursue my athletics career at the same time. I was so close to my family, who had been there every step of the way growing up, but now I needed to learn to be independent and 'grow up'. I seemed to take it in my stride, just got on with it and didn't think too much about what could go wrong. I knew Anna would come with me, but I thought that she wouldn't bother me like she used to. We had almost come to a mutual agreement that I could break the rules to some extent but still hold on to a certain amount of control, and that would sustain our relationship.

Uni started well, and I joined the athletics team and got straight into a routine of training and studying, albeit very regimented and structured. Looking back, I can see how I was still under Anna's control. Nothing had changed. I forced myself to train twice a day without fail, and I would not deviate from my 'safe' foods. I managed to use the excuse that 'I was an athlete' if anyone ever asked why I wouldn't eat certain foods or why I was leaving the house at 5am, 7 days a week, to go and train.

Despite my first couple of weeks going ok, it soon became apparent that I wasn't welcome in the sports halls where I was staying. Maybe, I was vulnerable, maybe they could see I was not fitting in with them, maybe they did not like my routines, maybe they could see how strange my behaviours were, even though I kept to myself. They soon became nasty and malicious and began a campaign of verbal bullying. At the time I was not aware that it was a case of bullying. I had been such a confident and popular girl as a young child. I had never experienced anything like this before, so I just assumed they were a bit nasty, tried to ignore it, it was nothing serious. I was 18 years old, surely bullying didn't happen at university?

Back on the slippery slope

The bullying campaign only seemed to get worse, and I struggled to know what to do. I began to feel anxious, feeling like I was not welcome, not good enough. I soon found myself trying to control my food intake again, restricting, cutting foods out of my diet and scanning every label of food products in the store. I did lost connection with feelings and emotions again, however I recognised that I felt I had little control over my life, and food was something to fill that void. It was something that I could focus on, something to distract me from the emotions I didn't want to feel. Foods I deemed 'unhealthy' were off-limits, my portion sizes decreased, and I was back in a strong relationship with Anna. I added extra training to my days and was skipping lectures to complete additional exercise sessions. Anorexia had taken a firm hold again.

I was returning home each weekend to spend time with my family. It was only a 45-minute drive on a good run. Every time I arrived; I could see the looks of concern on my family's faces when they saw me. I tried to pretend I didn't notice. I didn't let on that there was a problem, just explained I was training hard, and things were going fine. Although I did tell them I was having some struggles with the other students in my flat. My sister showed much concern for me, but I refused to engage with her. She tried to show me love and support, but I just continued to push her as far away as possible. I didn't mean to. It was Anna who was turning me into a malicious and spiteful girl, not the Jen everyone once knew.

Weeks went by, and weight was gradually falling off me. I also obtained a bad injury, which meant I couldn't run. Being anorexic, exercise was something I depended on. It was something I had to do to earn any food that passed my lips. Not being able to run led to a heightening of my anxiety. I needed to exercise. I could not rest. Rest for any anorexic is considered lazy. So I compensated by doubling the amounts of anything I could still do. I was swimming every day, doing endless exercise in my bedroom until I would finally collapse on my bed, exhausted and weak. But I still maintained the rhetoric that I needed to do this, *'I was an athlete'*.

By this stage, I could feel my bones digging into the mattress. I struggled to find a comfortable position in which to rest. I would toss and turn at night, not laying on one side for too long otherwise, I would be in too much pain. Anna had convinced however these pains were a sign on me 'winning'. Where in fact, now I understand, the winner of anorexia is the first one to die. It was not long after this time that my parents decided to pull me out of university. They saw their daughter disappearing in front of their eyes. Deep down, I think I wanted to pull out too, I couldn't cope, but I needed someone else to take the choice out of my hands. Even so, I felt like such a failure.

The following week my parents and I went to the flat to clear my room. Together we walked up the stairs along the corridor to find something we were not expecting, something so nasty and cruel. My flat mates had cut letters out of newspapers to create words to stick on my door saying*:*

'FLAT FOR SALE, THANK GOODNESS SHE IS GONE, GOOD RIDDANCE'.

I burst into tears, and mum nestled me in her arms while my dad's face spoke anger and rage. He stormed down to the reception area, where he found a staff member (who had previously refused to acknowledge that this was a case of bullying). He politely requested she come upstairs to witness this cruel act. She accepted this request and when she arrived at the top of the stairs her expression changed completely. She looked aghast, and I even noticed a tear fall down her cheek.

"I am so sorry," she muttered.

Dad responded, *"It's a bit late. However I would just make sure something gets put in place for the next person to arrive in this room with these people."*

With that we collected my things and left campus to make our way back home, home with my family again.

Taken to rock bottom

The next few years of my life would be described as a complete nightmare. An existence of a lost lifeless soul, getting progressively weaker. Taken to the depths of despair and with no idea what to do. Anorexia had taken complete control. I was fading, slowly falling into a very dark place. I became even more malicious, a horrible girl to be in the presence of. I never broke a smile, all I cared about was adhering to Anna's rules. Days out with family and friends could not happen anymore. I would avoid all family celebrations, choosing to stay at home and exercise instead. I avoided family holidays, holidays that once brought so much happiness and joy to my life. I created excuses not to attend an appointment or event that got in the way of Anna's rules.

One of my biggest regrets was my decision to take myself away to Australia for Christmas; on my own to get away from all the family celebrations. A trip that means I could escape from all the Christmas food, the change to routine and the celebrations that would disrupt my exercise routine. I needed an excuse to be able to adhere to Anna's rules. So, without telling anyone, I booked a trip to Australia. I booked myself into some of the most expensive hotels, because that was the only way I felt confident I would have all the requirements Anna and I would need, gyms, swimming pools, foods I would eat. I pretended to family and friends that this was what I really wanted to do, but it wasn't. It was the craziest thing Anna did to me.

No 20-year-old girl in her right mind travels to the other side of the world on her own to spend Christmas Day in a five-star apartment eating salad, spending hours in the gym, and walking aimlessly around Sydney? I chose to isolate myself from every other person in the world on New

Year's Eve to spend it alone eating vegetables and doing star jumps in my bedroom, before collapsing, falling into a deep sleep at 9.30pm, to be woken by my alarm at 5.30am the next day for the gym? This is what anorexia does. It doesn't care about anything you love. It doesn't care about the joy, fun and life that you miss out on. Eating disorders are torture, robbing you of every last drop glimmer of happiness. Eating disorders convince you to make the most irrational thoughts rational, regardless of your level of intelligence.

My family were speechless when they found out what I did and horrified when I'd told them of my plans. Firstly, they were hurt that their daughter wouldn't spend Christmas with them, but they were also petrified about what would happen to me while I was away. Would I even survive the trip, or would Anna claim my life? But what could they do? I remember my sister was angry at my parents about it.

"Are you crazy?" She shouted. *"You're just going to let her go on this trip? That is ridiculous! I can't even look at her right now."*

But my parents didn't really have any option; I was an adult and had free will. I used to love Christmas as a child. My family tried so desperately to remind me of this, of all the wonderful memories we had created together every year, all the fun and laughter. But I just shouted back at them, telling them I had changed, and I didn't enjoy it anymore and just wanted to experience something different for Christmas. It was terrifying how Anna would create so many lies, manipulate my brain and make me conform to all the terrible rules just to get me through each day.

I remember the trip to Australia so well, but all for the wrong reasons. I was about to visit one of the most incredible countries in the world. A place every teenager wants to see, to travel around with friends, staying in hostels and coming home having had the best experience and created the most incredible memories. However, I would not get to experience this. I went solo and spent my days walking aimlessly on my own, trying to convince myself I was having a great time, but unable to appreciate this amazing country. Rather than embracing all on offer, I was so focused on how much exercise I was doing, the food I was eating, the rules of anorexia. My mind was constantly plagued each day. I planned every outing around when I would exercise and where I would eat. I made sure I didn't sit down all day apart from at mealtimes, pushing my body to complete exhaustion.

On Christmas Day, I woke up to my normal grueling exercise session before sitting down to my one poached egg and vegetables for breakfast. I opened the presents Mum had packed for me, on my own, in my apartment, trying to convince myself this was what I wanted. The rest of the day, I spent out walking on my own while watching families celebrate together on the beach, having BBQs, laughing, and joking. Part of me dreamt of being able to do that, but that dream was drowned by Anna's voice telling me I didn't need that, I only needed her, and that was enough. We were a team.

I came home from the trip and tried to convince both myself and everyone else around me that I'd had an amazing time. But deep within, I knew I hadn't and while no one questioned my behavior and the odd decision to travel alone over Christmas, no one challenged me. They just nodded and agreed.

Over the next year I continued to deteriorate. I was isolating myself from everyone by this point. I spent no time with the few friends I had left, avoided my family as much as possible and I was still managing to spend two hours every morning in the gym, before going to my part-time job as a teaching assistant. I'd told the school I couldn't work mornings. I lied and told them I taught gym classes, to ensure I could get my exercise in and then I would finish work at 3.30pm which was perfect for me to get another exercise session in at home before a 5.30pm dinner. Times and schedules became extremely rigid and had to be maintained to the precise minute. I would cook a tiny fillet of fish and steamed vegetables before pursuing another exercise session in my bedroom because I could not stand the thought of having food inside of me. I had to get rid of it somehow.

This was how life continued, every day, exactly the same. A waste of years that I could have been enjoying myself and creating a positive future for myself. All the while, Anna tried to convince me this was how I wanted my life to be and continued to whisper in my ear that I was doing well. I was getting 'stronger'. It was, in fact, quite the opposite. I was a manipulative lifeless soul. Lost and slowly losing her chance of any life. A girl who grew up with so much life, energy, and talent. A girl who was adventurous, exciting, and sassy. All of which had now disappeared, it was gone completely, I was unrecognizable.

My family were increasingly concerned for my health but also for my life. They could see me slipping away each day, and it broke their hearts to see their 22 year old daughter struggling to find the energy to even walk up the stairs. Picking my legs up was exhausting. They were like heavyweights, but Anna continued to drive me to push through. I was still pushing myself through exercise sessions too, but always early in the morning as this was the only time I could find some sort of energy to get through. I couldn't run anymore though, the girl who once dreamed of being an Olympic athlete, who had so much potential, who lived and breathed running, could no longer pick her legs up to even consider running.
One day I tried, I went for a walk in my village, and tried to start running. I tried to pick up one leg and put it in front of the other. Something that came so naturally to me before, yet now seemed impossible. I physically couldn't lift them. I was losing my fight. At times I would find brief moments where I wanted to fight and challenge Anna, but I just couldn't do it.

I was completely lost. I wanted to give her my body, my life. I had had enough. It was at the desperate time my parents and sister visited my doctor. They pleaded with him, begging him to help. My sister sobbed in front of him, trying to explain that I would die if nobody could help me. But the doctor said unless I went to see him there was nothing he could do, though he said he would write a letter requesting to see me. When the letter arrived in the post a few days later, I quickly found it before Mum did, tore it to shreds and hid it in the bottom of the bin. A couple of weeks later, I got another one reminding me to book to see the doctor. I once again threw this in the bin. Another two weeks later another one arrived, and this time I wasn't the first to see the post. Mum found it before me, and she made sure this letter wasn't going to pass us by. She booked an appointment and then quite literally had to drag me to the clinic to see the doctor.

By this point, the doctor could see how poorly I was and sent me straight to a consultant, who referred me to his colleague at a specialist hospital for eating disorders. I remember feeling so angry that Mum was forcing me to visit these doctors, but at the same time, Anna was convincing me that I would be able to lie my way through this. I would be able to persuade these people I was fine and would then just carry on the way I was. That had served me well until now, so why would this be any different? Everyone was trying to make me see how unwell I was, how my organs would go into failure, how I would die if I didn't accept treatment. But Anna and I refused to listen, to anyone.

Life as an inpatient

It was 7pm on a Friday just before the Easter break. I was sitting in the eating disorder inpatient hospital with Mum, waiting to see an eating disorder psychiatrist to assess me. We sat in silence. I wasn't talking to her; I was so angry with her. The door of the doctor's room opened. I remember feeling petrified the instant I saw the consultant and the stern look on her face, with little trace of empathy or kindness. She invited us into the room and straight away asked to weigh me, after which she gave a serious glare. She advised me I would be admitted as an inpatient as soon as a bed was available. Until that time, she said I would be a day patient.

My heart felt like it stopped, it was almost as if time stopped for a brief moment. I sat aghast, trying to comprehend what she just said. But I still felt that somehow, I would be able to get out of this. I knew I needed to act fast, I had to say something. I had to convince her she was wrong. I needed her to believe I was fine, I was not sick, I did not need her help.

"Please give me another chance. I will eat more, I promise. I don't need to be in hospital," I begged her.

She replied with little empathy: *"There are no ifs and buts. I have worked with many people like you, you are very sick. There is no option but to be admitted, and if you refuse, we shall have to section you."*

Section me? I didn't even know what that was, but it sounded pretty serious. Mum and I were both bawling our eyes out. I was quite hysterical, Mum tried to hug me, and I pushed her away. But she remained firm and agreed with the doctor.

"Jennifer, listen. You have to do this. You need to get better."

The doctor told Mum to drop me off at the hospital at 7am the following day, and to pick me up at 7pm. This would continue until a bed became available for me to be an inpatient. The rest of that evening remains very unclear in my mind, it was as if my mind was spinning the entire time until I managed to fall asleep, which was very early hours of the morning. Why were these people being so mean? They were about to ruin my relationship with Anna, my only friend, for so long. How could I maintain my relationship with her when I could not adhere to her food and exercise rules? Although, while I was having all these irrational thoughts, at the same time there was a very small part of me that was slightly relieved that someone else was going to take over my fight. I was petrified and didn't know how I would manage this. But at this stage I had no choice.

The next morning, I got up very early, before the rest of my family. I needed to get an exercise session done in my bedroom as I wasn't able to go to the gym. I was no longer allowed to drive because the doctor said my health was at risk and she had suspended my driver's license. I made sure I was quiet and managed to fit in an hour of exercise to burn off as much as possible, doing anything I could to hold on to my relationship with Anna. At 6.30am, just as I crawled up on to my feet from finishing my final set of endless sit-ups mum came into my room to say we needed to leave. I was still refusing to speak to her or anyone else in my family. I ignored my sister and my dad as we left the house. The journey consisted of mum and I sat in silence all the way to the hospital, which felt like it was never-ending.

On arrival, mum signed me in, and we were advised to walk to the inpatient unit. I remember walking in and seeing all these sick patients, everyone staring at me. It was clear within an instant how things went in the ward. A new patient arrives, and everyone would be intrigued to see who the latest person was to enter what was considered torture in the inpatient unit. Lifeless souls would stare, and in that moment it was as if we had an inner connection that read;

I feel you, I know how you feel and I know you feel so misunderstood. I am with you.
I realised I was the new one, but it didn't feel right... these people looked sick. I wasn't like them. I didn't look sick like them... surely, I didn't? But I was sick, I did look sick, of course, I did, I just couldn't see it at the time. Looking back at photos of myself around this time, I can see I was extremely unwell and can only describe my appearance as an old lady, with a shrivelled-up face, hair falling out, and my skin ghostly white. A young girl aged 22 with the appearance of an 80 year-old, unrecognizable.

Mum was advised to kiss me goodbye and leave me to be called for breakfast. Tears fell down her face as she wrapped her arms around my bony body and kissed me on the cheek.

"I love you so, so much, darling. I will see you tonight," she whispered in my ear.

I began to weep, and tears streamed down my face as I watched her walk away. She couldn't look back; she knew she had to leave me.

I was first sent for my preliminary assessment with the doctor, who weighed me first and then did an ECG, confirming how critical I was. My bloods were taken, and results were back within a few hours, confirming I had a white blood count of 0.2 (a minimum for healthy is a level of 4), sex hormones were non-existent, inflammation markers were elevated, and I was deficient in nearly every nutrient. I was described and documented; a critical case.

The next thing I knew, I was called by the nurse to join the others for breakfast.

"Jennifer, please come through to the kitchen."

I was horrified as I walked in and saw other patients sitting with bowls of cereal swamped in milk and a plate next to each bowl with two slices of butter- and jam-laden toast and in front of that a glass of fruit juice. There was no way on this earth I was going to be eating something like that. No way! These people were just trying to make us fat, feeding us all this food. This was what Anna was telling me, but obviously that was not the goal of inpatient treatment.

I trembled as I sat myself at the end of the table. Petrified as to what would be put in front of me.

"Weetabix or Frosties, Jennifer?", the nurse asked.

"I don't want either of those, thank you. Can I just have some porridge with almond milk, please? Just a little, I'm not that hungry," I replied with some confidence I would get what I requested.

The nurse looked over and laughed.

"Jennifer, you are here for a reason, and that is to recover from an eating disorder. You are not here to tell us what you want. These are your two options."

I stared at her, blank, unsure how I was going to get around this one.

"Erm, Weetabix then, please, but with almond milk, please, I don't like cow's milk (which was another lie)," I hesitantly replied.

"Jennifer, we don't allow almond milk. You are having Weetabix with cow's milk," the nurse snapped and walked

away, promptly returning with the breakfast, which she placed in front of me.

I stared at the bowl, and my whole body began to tremble again. The bowl was full of milk, and, underneath, hidden, were two Weetabix. I was petrified and needed to find a way to avoid as much of this breakfast as possible. I watched: everyone around the table was shaking just like me, but all of them slowly began to eat. There was no conversation. Everyone was in the midst of their own internal battles at this point, battles with the voice in their head telling them they were a failure and letting themselves down, that they must not eat, nor listen to the staff who were making them eat. But they clearly knew the consequences if they didn't, which I was yet to learn.

I slowly began to eat.

A breakfast that as a child I loved left me feeling disgusted in myself and like I was a complete failure. I tried my best to drain off as much milk as possible, but the nurse soon caught on and told me to stop. I felt worse and worse with each mouthful, my anxiety increasing with every bite. I stopped halfway through and said I was finished. The nurse asked me to eat some more, but I refused, thinking that would be fine. She put this yellow-coloured milk drink in front of me. I asked her what it was.

"For all the food you leave, we make up for it with a Fortisip supplement drink, and if you refuse this, you will be tubed instantly," she replied.

I stared at her blankly. I couldn't quite make sense of everything. It felt like I was in prison with orders to obey. Ironically this was the internal experience that I had suffered with anorexia for the past 10 years, obeying Anna's rules, consumed in a prison of my own mind and body. I realised, however, that I had to drink this, there was no way I wanted to be 'tubed'. Tears streamed down my face as my hand once again trembled, and I picked up the glass to drink the thick, sickly milk drink. Surprisingly, I did manage to finish it, but only after a 30-minute battle inside my mind and with the nurse.

After breakfast, my thoughts instantly turned to the fact that I now needed to exercise to get rid of all that food. I asked to go to the garden for a walk. The nurse looked at me.

"No Jennifer. You are in supervision now for an hour, so go and sit in the lounge and watch TV, or read a book," she said.

I felt the greatest sense of fear creep over me. How could I possibly sit for an hour and vegetate and be *'lazy'*? I couldn't possibly commit to that. I walked into the lounge and stood against the wall. The nurse pointed to the sofa.

"Oh no," I said, *"I'm ok, thanks, I'll stand."*

She replied with force: *"Jennifer, we are not having any of these games. Sit down like everyone else."*

My eyes welled with tears, not only because I was disobeying Anna but also because I've never liked getting in trouble or people being angry with me. I perched myself on the edge of the sofa and closed my eyes, hoping to be swallowed up into a dark place where I no longer had to deal with any of this. Sitting down for an hour is no task at all for any healthy person, instead probably a welcomed rest. For someone with anorexia, this is a task that creates significant anxiety, fear and discomfort. Discomfort beyond describable.

When the hour had passed, I asked to go to the garden for some fresh air (when really, I was planning to exercise in a place where I could hide). But although I was granted permission, I soon noticed I was not alone; one of the nurses was coming with me. As we got to the garden, she told me to sit on the bench.

"Can I walk around the garden, please?", I pleaded.

"No, you must sit down, please," she quickly responded. I argued back: *"But I have just been sitting for the past hour. I need to walk."*

She simply repeated that I must do as I was told, or we'd just have to go back inside. I sat my bottom down on the bench, put my head in my hands and tried to think of a way to escape this place. I couldn't come back here tomorrow. This was simply not going to work.

Lunchtime soon came around and I, along with the rest of the patients, walked into the kitchen. All of us lifeless souls, buried under layers of baggy clothes to hide our skeletal frames (as well as to keep us warm). I sat down, and the nurse put a plate in front of me with tinfoil over the top. She removed the foil, and my mouth dropped open; my heart pounded. She had given me a sandwich. My mind was spinning. Bread terrified me, the food that diet culture has villainized, the food I had avoided for so many years, the food Anna made me believe I never wanted to eat again? I took the top piece of bread off to see what was inside. Butter! Butter was spread thickly on the bread and in between the slices was ham. My thoughts were completely irrational but this demonstrates how all-consuming eating disorders become and how skewed your mind becomes It convinces you of the craziest things, a sandwich, the staple lunchtime delicacy across many countries of the world was something I had become terrified of, which was only exacerbated by the messages from diet culture in society.

I told the nurse I couldn't eat this, and we went through the same battles that we'd had at breakfast. The lunch period finished with me in tears on the floor screaming like a toddler having a tantrum. I was told that because I only ate half the sandwich and tried to wipe off butter and hide it by wiping it under the table, I must have a whole carton of Fortisip. These battles continued for the remainder of the day as I pushed my luck during supervisions and tried to manipulate the nurses. Trying to find any way I could to burn off calories, refusing to drink milk at snack time and then arguing my way through dinner, at which I refused to eat anything apart from the vegetables on my plate. I was not touching pasta and Bolognese sauce.

During my final supervision for the day, my eyes were consistently on the clock, counting the seconds until Mum would arrive. I was working out in my head how I was going to convince her not to bring me back tomorrow. There was no way I could disobey Anna for more than one day. I needed to get back to her rules. The clock struck 7pm, and I saw Mum walk through the door at the end of the corridor. Despite not speaking to her when she dropped me off, I had never felt so grateful to see her. I threw myself into her arms as she approached me and burst into tears.

She looked at the nurse and asked, *"Has she been, ok?"*

"It's been a struggle," the nurse replied. *"And she has not been responding well to eating, but we will try again tomorrow."*

I turned to her and muttered, *"I won't be coming back tomorrow."*

I turned and raced down the corridor and to the car. On the way home I begged and pleaded with Mum not to take me back, but she was not backing down. She knew she needed to be cruel to be kind to me now because if she didn't, I would die. I cried all the way home, and for the rest of the night before, I finally cried myself to sleep. Little did I know that would be the last night in my own bed for a very long time.

The day my freedom was taken away

Even now, thinking about that day, the 5th of April 2015, the day my parents left me at the inpatient unit – leaves me feeling cold and terrified. I arrived for my day-patient treatment, but as we entered the unit, we were informed that a bed had become available. Mum and I were advised that I would be admitted that day and due to me being documented "a critical case", I would be under 24-hour supervision by a nurse. Mum had to leave me there to go home to pack a bag for me, and I had to stay at the hospital. I was now officially an inpatient, my name written on the inpatient board with all the others who were fighting their own battles. Some days names would be rubbed off, for one of two reasons. Either the individual had successfully managed to recover enough to be discharged. Or, more tragically, some would lose their fight all together.

I remember sitting on my bed, thinking that this wasn't real. How could I be in an eating disorder inpatient unit with all of my freedom taken away? How could it have come to this? I wanted to be back as Jen, the athlete, running free. I didn't believe I was ill enough to be in hospital. I didn't believe I was like the rest of the patients in there; they were really ill, I was just struggling a little. I pleaded with my nurse. I begged her. I promised my consultant I would try harder if she let me go home. It was pointless. I sat on the edge of my bed. I cried for hours until I finally fell asleep with the nurse carefully watching my every move for the next 12 hours before I would wake at 6am to experience my first full day as an inpatient.

I woke the following day before 6am, and the nurse sitting by my bed instructed me straight to the weigh-in room. I looked puzzled to begin with, still a little sleepy, but I soon realised this would be a daily routine. I walked down the dark corridor to join the back of the queue; girls lined up with hollow faces, no expression, just empty souls who were existing in what felt like a prison.

"Next," a lady shouted!

The next girl in the queue walked into the room. As she entered and the door closed, I could hear her shouting and yelling to the nurse.

"No, I have been trying, I promise I have been trying… please don't put me on a tube, please, please… I HATE YOU! I HATE YOU ALL! YOU'RE ALL SO MEAN. YOU'RE JUST TRYING TO MAKE ME FAT," she cried.

The girl then stormed out of the weigh-in room sobbing and scurried back to her room before slamming the door so hard the building walls shook.

"What just happened?", I whispered to the girl behind me.

"She lost weight again, so they are going to tube her," she replied with a sad expression. She responded to my confused expression, elaborating: *"You know… they will put a tube through her nose and feed her like that. So, she has no choice but to consume crazy amounts of calories."*

At this point, I had never been so petrified in all my life. I was next to walk in. What if they said the same to me? I could not allow myself to be fed with lots of calories. I didn't need them.

"Next!" came a voice from inside the weigh-in room.

I tiptoed my way slowly towards the door and poked my head around.

"Come on, we haven't got all day. Undress and stand on the scales, please," the nurse demanded.

I took my pyjamas off and crept over to the set of scales placed in front of me. I slowly stepped on and turned my gaze to the lady. She was shaking her head.

She made a brief comment: *"Oh dear, not in a good way, not good at all."*

With that, she told me to get dressed and leave.

I was happy. Well, Anna was happy. I had clearly managed to lose more weight and I had not been told I would be tube-fed. With that I thought maybe this inpatient stint would be easier than I first thought. I had so many tricks up my sleeve I was certain I could deceive or manipulate the staff in here to believe I was fine.

When I went back to my room, the head nurse of the acute ward, the ward I was on came in to explain how inpatient treatment would work. My target weight was set, and it was explained to me the three stages of treatment, an acute treatment where they would aim to stabilize me and start me on my weight gain plan. Stage 2 would be progression, where I began to have a bit more freedom and flexibility. But this had to be earned. Lastly, transition where you were given the freedom to prepare and cook your own meals, but if you lost weight or were seen to be presenting with behaviours associated with your eating disorder, you would drop back down to progression or acute. The whole aim was to restore weight and then be at a place to maintain it. There would be some psychological support, but this was an area that the hospital failed on. During this meeting, she also gave me a document which was titled care plan, it outlined the targets that had been set for me. A schedule of mealtimes, supervision after meals, and the rules to be adhered to. Some of these rules included no exercising, no chewing gum, no moving around during supervision, no going to the toilet during supervision after meals, no diet drinks, no low-fat foods, three meals and three snacks to be consumed every day, 45-minute limits for mealtimes, no-calorie burning postures such as standing, fidgeting or tapping feet whilst sitting down, no separation of foods during mealtimes.

It felt like rules that would be provided in prison, not in hospital. I began to fear how I would possibly be able to sneak exercise into my daily routine whilst my every move being watched, or how would I sneak food off my plate. But I hoped that somehow Anna and I would come up with a plan.

Just like my day-patient treatment, there was no escaping the food they were about to feed me, and this time it was worse than before. At 8.30am, there was a loud call from the kitchen for breakfast. Panic consumed me. I had no idea what would be given to me; they had informed me it would be slightly different now I was an inpatient and could be monitored 24 hours a day, and my nutrition adjusted accordingly. Still, I just tried to convince myself it was fine. I would eat a couple of mouthfuls and leave the rest.

I once again made the long, slow walk down the dark corridor to the kitchen. As I entered the room, the other girls turned their heads. It felt like they tried to smile at me and be friendly to the new girl, but it was as if they just didn't even have the energy to break into a smile. All were hunched over the table, looking anxious. Some were shaking, some were already crying. I sat myself down, and the nurse placed my breakfast in front of me. Like before, it was two Weetabix soaked in milk, but this time with the addition of a banana, a slice of toast and what I considered to be a mountain of peanut butter. I looked at the nurse.

"Excuse me," I muttered. *"I don't think you've given me the right breakfast. Are you sure this is mine?"*

"Jen, of course, it's yours," she said. *"You have 45 minutes."*

I sat and stared. My head was spinning with uncontrollable thoughts, anger, confusion, frustration. All the while, I tried to muster up a plan to somehow get away without eating this breakfast. My hand was shaking, but I managed to grasp the spoon, and I hovered it above the Weetabix. I put a small amount on the spoon and pressed it against the bowl like I'd done before, attempting to get rid of as much milk as I could, and then I slowly put it towards my lips. I looked up to see if she was watching and met her eyes, peering down at me. I slowly put the food in my mouth and just held it there. At this point, with the nurse staring over me, I realised I wasn't going to be able to escape this time. It suddenly hit me: Anna was not going to win this battle and stop me from eating this breakfast. I was somehow going to have to sit there and finish it. I tried to hold as much milk in my mouth as I could, waiting for a moment she wasn't looking to try and spit it back into the bowl, but it wasn't going to work. She knew what I was doing. I wondered whether I could scoop it into my pockets somehow, down my trousers, under the table, anywhere, anywhere but my mouth.

"Don't be holding that milk in your mouth. You have to finish everything in that bowl, and you know what happens if you don't," the nurse instructed.

At the end of the 45 minutes, I had reluctantly eaten the Weetabix and half the banana but not touched the toast. I refused to eat bread; the thought terrified me. Anna had convinced me that bread was something never to pass my lips, which was tied up in my fear of carbohydrates, something diet culture had led me to believe. I got up to leave but was swiftly called back.

"Jen, where do you think you're going? You need to have this supplement drink," the nurse called.

I looked down at the creamy milkshake drink waiting for me at the table – how could I forget that this was going to be given to me? I spent the next hour arguing with the nurse over the drink. Eventually, she won the battle. I hesitantly drank it.

After each meal all patients were ushered into the quiet lounge area to sit in supervision for an hour. It quite literally felt like I was in a care home for elderly people; everyone sitting in chairs looking lifeless, sad, and staring into space. The nurse would sit with us and watch us like a hawk. If we were caught fidgeting, tapping our feet or standing up, we were instantly told to sit still, sit down and not move. During this time, I understood why so many of us were struggling so much to break a smile. We were all sitting there enduring constant mental battles with Anna. Our brains consumed about the food we just ate and feeling disgusted with ourselves, feeling like we had failed Anna. There was nothing to distract us from these thoughts and no way to escape. It felt like complete torture, I just wanted it to end. I was ready to give up. I'd had enough of all of this; I couldn't see a future and I just wanted to let go.

At 10.30am, we were called back to the kitchen for snack time. This consisted of 250ml of whole milk and either a piece of fruit or a snack bar. If we chose the piece of fruit, we would have to have the snack bar later on with our afternoon snack. Despite me pleading to have fruit at both, this was not allowed. Often, I would choose the fruit in the morning with my milk. I was petrified of drinking milk, and the nurse had to sit next to me whilst I would shake with anxiety prompting me to drink it within the time limit.

After snack time, it would be another 30 minutes of supervision before we had our first period of some *"free time"*, if that's what you could call it. If you were not on full supervision, some patients would be able to sneak to their room to exercise without the nurse watching. But for me being on 24-hour watch, I had to sit with the anxiety, worry, panic and fear, with the nurse by my side. It was all consuming. I felt so lazy, fat and disgusted in myself. I felt such a traitor to Anna.

The rest of the day continued:

12.30 - 1.15 - Lunch

1.15 - 2.15 - Supervision

2.15 - 3.30 - Free time/ bed rest or therapy groups

3.30 - Snack time (250ml milk and a snack bar or fruit)

3.30 – 4.00 - Supervision

4.00 - 5.30 - Free time/ bed rest or therapy groups

5.30 - 6.30 - Dinner and dessert

6.30 - 7.30 - Supervision

7.30 – 9.00 - Free time or bed rest

9.00 - 9.30 - Snack (250ml milk & biscuits or a snack bar)

9.30 – 10.00 – Supervision

10.00 - Bedtime

This new routine quickly became the norm. Rigid rules, rigid structure, 24-hour monitoring, constant battles at mealtimes, and utter boredom. Meals were the hardest part; food being served, and I would sit with the constant battles in my head whilst the nurse would be prompting me to eat. As patients we used to judge each other, seeing who was eating what and who was managing to sneak food away or somehow fit in a bedroom exercise session.

It was at the point that I hit rock bottom. I felt like I had lost everything. I had lost Jen completely, and now my existence was trapped inside these four walls with no escape. The more I disobeyed Anna, the louder she shouted in my head, the more she told me I was a failure, I wasn't good enough, I wasn't worthy of life. My mind was in a constant battle that I could not escape.

Dear Mummy and Daddy,

When I look back over the years Anna has been in my life, I am so saddened by how I treated you both. How I disregarded your love, concern and care. The countless times I would tell you I would change, to only fall back into Anna's rules the following day. You brought me into this world, a miracle, innocent, adventurous, cheeky, a lover of life. You both gave me the best upbringing a child could have wished for. Yet, at that tender age of 12, Anna entered the scene. Please know you could not have prevented this from happening. I was destined to experience my time with Anna to bring me to where I am today. As hard as it is, as hard as it was, we must try now to see it as a blessing, despite the pain she caused us.

Thank you for saving my life, thank you for never giving up, thank you for loving me even when I said I hated you. I used to speak to you as though we were enemies, fighting on different teams. You were fighting for my life. You did everything to hold on to any glimpse of your daughter while I was fighting to remain in Anna's grip. Thank you for fighting my battles when I did not have the energy to. Thank you for choosing recovery before I could choose it myself. I do not think I will ever be able to express how so very sorry I am for all the years I brought Anna into our lives. How did you love me during that time of darkness, with an unwelcome imposter who ruled me, who ruined so many years, who robbed us of so many occasions that should have been filled with happy memories? But I know you understand this was not me. When I was sick, it was not me who said she hated you. It wasn't me who told infinite numbers of lies, it wasn't me who wanted to miss all the special family occasions and celebrations.

Anorexia turned me into a lifeless, vacant, spiteful,

malicious, and unloving person of myself. I can't even begin to imagine how hard it was for you both. To see me each day but not see Jen, the happy and loving little girl you brought into this world. To watch me slowly disappear before your eyes as I edged ever closer to death each day.

You fought for me every day. No matter how many times I refused to accept help, you never stopped battling because you knew that somewhere Jen was still inside. You pushed and pushed for me to be able to access treatment. You pleaded with the doctors to take care of me and to provide me with the treatment I needed. Time and time again, you were denied the support we needed, but you both continued to seek help. Sacrificing so much to save me. When I lost my voice and I was stuck in the dark hold of depression with no one but Anna dictating to me, you fought this intruder in my head yourselves, reminding me I was still there somewhere.

You both remained calm. You nurtured my soul to enable me to see the tiniest glimmer of hope. You helped me through countless meals where I wanted to back down and not challenge Anna, but you reminded me I could do it. You have both been my biggest advocates from the day I was born, to the day Anna came into my life. Through the darkest of days and all the way to now. You spent countless hours on my recovery, risking your own jobs to spend time with me at the hospital and taking me to appointment after appointment over the years. Every day of inpatient treatment, I would know that you would be there as soon as possible, coming to visit me, knowing how important it was that I see you.

In my eyes, my childhood was perfect, and I am so grateful for all the happy memories I have of my early days with you before Anna, even if some of them have been shaded from my brain. You couldn't have done anything more or anything different. I was meant to experience what I did, gain my scars; it was written in the stars the day I was born. It was the only way to lead me to my true purpose in this life.

We can never get all those years back that Anna robbed from us, but we can take from it that we are such an incredibly strong family because of what we worked through together. I quite simply would not be here today without everything you both did and do for me every day. Now is the time we can make up for time lost and create memories to treasure, but this time without Anna spoiling them. While I may never be that little Jen again, as I was before anorexia. I hope together we can learn to love and accept me even if I remain a little broken and bruised.

I love you now and always and forevermore.

Your little girl,

Jen

Cheesecake and cream

My existence continued, and I was slowly learning how to find ways to maintain my relationship with Anna while in the hospital. I had worked out who were the strict nurses and which ones I could manipulate; which ones wouldn't always watch me. The ones who would leave me for 5-10 minutes on my own in my bedroom, at which point I would do as much as I could to burn calories, star jumps, press-ups, sit-ups, anything I could. Before scurrying back to my bed just as she returned. If she ever caught me before I was lying down, I would say I needed to get something from my wardrobe. I remember one time; I was running on the spot as the nurse came in. I am sure to this day she saw me, or if she didn't, my face surely was a picture of guilt, but she didn't say anything.

I worked out which nurses not to sit next to at the dining table, as some would watch you eat every mouthful. While others may go on their phone, giving me the tiniest moment to be able to sneak some food off my plate and into my pocket, to later flush down the toilet to rid of any evidence. Every patient tried and tested everything they could to maintain their relationship with their eating disorder.

Weekends were always hardest, as some patients were allowed to go home if they were progressing well, so it was very lonely and boring. My parents and family were my savour as they would visit each day, but even then, we could not be alone, as I was always under a nurse's watch.

I was approaching the end of my first two weeks of inpatient treatment, having made little progress. There was no sign of me wanting to recover, no matter what my parents or the care team said. I was told that I was very close to organ failure. My immune system was failing, and my heart rate was worryingly low, which did startle me a little, but to Anna, this counted as success. The days consisted of constant battles – with myself, with Anna and with the staff. However, these first two weeks did stabilize me, and I was consuming some of the food I was given. I was still on quarter portions at that time due to a concern of refeeding me too quickly, which can be fatal. So, it felt somewhat manageable, even if I was finding some of the foods extremely challenging.

At the end of the second week, I was informed by my consultant I would be going up to half portions. I would now be required to eat a light dessert after lunch (e.g., a yogurt or rice pudding) and a main dessert after dinner (e.g., cheesecake and cream or sponge and custard). This terrified me, I was petrified about having to eat a dessert, as I knew it would be something that contained sugar. The last time I ate dessert was probably when I was 12 years old. It was definitely off-limits by Anna's rules. That evening I finished half of my dinner. I ate the vegetables and a fillet of salmon but refused to eat the rice. Then the nurse placed in front of me my dessert… lemon cheesecake hiding under a bowl of full cream. I was horrified. No way would I be eating that, I couldn't, I couldn't disobey Anna anymore. I sat there and began to cry, shaking with fear. The nurse sat next to me prompting me again, reminding me I had 20 minutes left to eat my food. But I couldn't do it. I battled with Anna in my head. I promised her that I would go back to her rules when I left but told her that she had to let me eat the cake now, just to get out of this prison. But it was no use. I gave in to her, I refused to eat and subsequently was forced a supplement ensure drink instead.

After arguing with the nurse over my glass of milk that evening and refusing to eat my cereal bar, I stumbled into my bedroom, crawled under the duvet, feeling like today had been an utter disaster on so many levels. I had failed Anna. I have failed myself, failed at everything. I closed my eyes, praying I would just go to sleep and the pain would be over. I prayed that my suffering could end, for my body to just let me rest now, to let Anna succeed. I was ready to let her win, I could not be her best friend anymore, and if I could not obey her rules, I could no longer carry on. I had lost all hope and was now at a point where I felt ready to give up on life. I didn't want to die, but Anna was making me not want to live. I was exhausted.

As I drifted off to sleep, I started to dream. It was a surreal dream, the kind that you remember forever, one that remains so clear in my mind to this day. I dreamt of myself living my happiest life. I was that happy young girl again, the girl who was cheeky and precocious, who excelled at school. I was top of the class at sport but wasn't so great at art. The girl who was sassy and adventurous but a little stubborn and would sulk if she didn't get her own way. The girl who adored running and loved the feeling of the wind in her hair. The girl who was free, laughing and smiling with friends, family and loved ones. As I dreamt of this happy time in my life, I had a visit in my dream from my nan, who had passed a few years prior. She only appeared briefly, but she whispered in my ear.

"Keep going, darling. You are so brave, and you have more to bring to this world than you will ever know. Trust the process, darling girl. Do not give up on this. There is a life waiting for you. I love you dearly, I believe in you, I know you can do this."

I remember waking up and looking around the room before coming to the realization that it wasn't real. It was a dream. However, something at that moment felt strange and different. I can't explain the feeling that came over me. I had spent so long battling, unable to see daylight, unable to leave the shore and take the challenge of venturing out to sea. But that morning, I finally found the smallest amount of courage and this weird feeling of knowing that maybe, just maybe, part of me did want to get better. Part of me wanted to get to experience what life had to offer. To this day, I struggle to comprehend how overnight, after so many years, I managed to find the smallest glimmer of hope that I wanted to recover. Whether it was influenced by the dream or from the realization of what Anna was doing to me after spending the first two weeks in hospital, I will never know. But what was sure was that I was starting to think that perhaps I could prepare myself to do whatever it took to get what I wanted and make sure that my life was worth living. For the first time in as long as I could remember, I was able to begin to articulate a desire to recover.

I think for the first time, I began to see Anna had never really been my friend. She was manipulating me, she was slowly destroying me, my life, the life of others around me. She made me believe that she was helping me, that I could not be without her, but she wasn't. She had taken everything away from me. I was a 22-year-old sat in hospital having lost out on so much from the age of 12. I should have been out in the world, creating my future, partying, socializing, working, dating, everything a 22-year-old should be able to do. However, even though I acknowledged this, I couldn't let her go just yet. I still felt I needed her to hold me, to make me feel safe in this world. Part of me still wanted her to be with me every day.

But how could I recover if I allowed her to stay?

Challenging Anna

The following morning, I walked into breakfast and sat myself down. I still felt nervous, my whole body was still shaking as it did at every meal or snack, and part of me felt like pulling out of what I had just committed to. I really wasn't sure I could do this. But deep down inside, I managed to find a tiny glimmer of hope and trust, and I knew I wanted this. I couldn't give up on life just yet. My breakfast was put in front of me; two Weetabix with milk, 1 slice of toast with peanut butter and a banana. I took a deep breath, closed my eyes, and took my first mouthful. The emotions I felt that morning were a little different though. For the first time in longer than I could remember, I felt like I had given myself some permission to eat. With that permission there was a part of me that was finally able to enjoy the taste of the food, indulge in the textures, scents and colours that sat before me. I slowly worked my way through the meal. The nurse looked over, giving me those doubtful eyes. I knew she thought that she might catch me trying to find ways to get rid of my food again. Anna was screaming at me in that moment and there was a big part of me wanting to give into her, to try to eliminate as much of my breakfast as I could, to obey her rules. Her voice nagging me to scoop some into my pocket during that brief moment, the nurse turned her back. But I didn't listen. I battled that voice, I held my own, I ate my breakfast.

I finished my last mouthful of toast, and I experienced a huge sense of achievement and pride. The nurse gazed over.

"Well done, Jen," she said, giving me a small, sweet smile, and at that point, I knew that she must have seen this time and time again when a patient finally turns the corner. It

was by no means easy. Recovery was never going to be easy, it is not linear, and it is a long journey with many twists and turns. Recovery is messy, and there was still a long way to go, but I had made a firm start on the path to get there.

The next few days felt exhausting. It was constant work, and my mind was twisted in battles at every meal. Yet with every bite, I just kept reminding myself that this was helping me. All the time, Anna was trying so hard to stop me, to make me go back to her rules. She persistently tried to convince me I was a failure and a traitor and tried to remind me that I needed her. However, I used all my energy to shut out that voice; I knew I wanted to get better. I ate everything I was given. I started to hit my weekly targets, gaining 1kg every time. As a result, I was rewarded with some time with my family, which was so special for me. Mum, Dad and Jo had been there without fail every afternoon to visit me, and the day we were allowed to spend 20 minutes outside without supervision from a nurse felt incredible. Sitting on a bench for 20 minutes in the garden – something that had felt like torture when I first arrived – now felt like freedom and brought me so much happiness. More importantly for me, for the first time in a very long time, I was able to feel genuine love for my family again, as Anna had taken a bit of a back seat, she was still very much with me, but for brief moments each day, I managed to shut her out just for a while. As the weeks went on, this free time progressed to small day trips with my family and eventually a full weekend to spend at home together. All of this was on the provision that I would stick to my meal plan and return to my weigh-in the following week, still having achieved my 1kg target.

I finally started to feel I was seeing real glimmers of myself coming back. My family were seeing glimmers of Jen again. I could see their smiles also returning. They almost lost me, but now they were seeing me starting to regain life and get stronger. I had visions of my future, returning to sport and being the athlete, I had always dreamed of becoming, and this motivated me every day. I was a girl on a mission and was determined to succeed. Weekends spent with my family at home had changed dramatically, from me avoiding food in every way I could to now being more worried that I wasn't going to consume enough. I was scared to return to the hospital, having failed to gain my 1kg, so I would often go a little over on the meal plan because I was so adamant, I had to reach the target. It was strange. I couldn't remember the last time my family had seen me eat a 'normal meal' without refusing it, shouting, crying or arguing. They looked at me with encouragement and pride, knowing I was working so hard to try to recover. The battles in my head were there, but I was so focused at this time, I was able to override Anna for the first time in many years. I would remind myself at every meal that I was one meal closer to home, one meal closer to freedom, one meal closer to life.

A fragile diagnosis

The following week I ward round. This consisted of a progression review, where each patient would tremble as they sat in a room with the treatment team. It would be decided whether to reward you and let you progress or remove freedom if you have not been complying with treatment. This used to be a day full of so many mixed emotions on the ward. One patient would come out swearing, screaming, and smashing their head against walls, and you knew instantly they had experienced a bad ward round. While the next might come out smiling tentatively as they had been progressed from the acute ward to the progression ward, where they received a little more freedom. For me, this week's ward round left me empty, numb and confused. Not because I hadn't been complying, I was doing well. I was gaining weight each week and complying with my meal plan and the hospital rules. I was still unable to do any exercise, but I was no longer on constant watch by the nurse. They just made sure they kept an eye on me. I would be lying to say that my obsession with exercise had faded. Despite my compliance to eating my meal plan, I still found myself needing to burn food off to feel ok with what I was eating. I started to become obsessed with the idea of obtaining a 'fit' physique. I remember saying to my family I didn't mind gaining weight if I looked fit. This I later found out was something many individuals become obsessed with during recovery, obtaining the "strong not skinny" look. Which may sound harmless, however it is simply swapping one obsession for another, and from experience I know it can be just as harmful as restrictive forms of anorexia.

Walking into my ward round, I had a smile on my face because I knew I had been doing well. My consultant commented on these facts and emphasized how proud she was. She also mentioned that my inpatient stay may be shorter than we'd once thought if I continued this way. However, she gazed down at the table looking at a piece of paper in front of her.

"Jen, I have your bone scan results here, and I am afraid it's not good news. You have severe osteoporosis of the spine and the hips, and are at an extremely high risk of fracture," she explained.

I sat for a moment, my face a blank. Silently working through what she had just said to me. At first, I told myself it could not be true. How could I have osteoporosis, I was an athlete? I began to cry.

"I'm sorry, Jen. The years without having your menstrual cycle, a lack of sex hormones, and extensive malnourishment means that your bones are not holding up very well. However, Jen, if you act now, we can partially reverse this," my consultant continued

I couldn't believe it.

"Partially? You mean I can't get rid of this completely?" I questioned.

She shook her head, *"I'm afraid not, Jen."*

I felt my whole body go numb. Growing up, I always felt that when I'd made mistakes in life, it always seemed you would get a second chance. You could always try again. But now, for the first time in my life, I had to accept that I would not get a second chance with this. I would not be able to have the bones of a 23-year-old like I wished. I had to accept that I would always have weaker bones than I should. I sat sobbing, I felt all of my motivation seep out of me. I realised how much impact the years of this cruel and entrenching illness had wrought on my body. I began to hate Anna even more than I already did. She was not my friend. She was never my friend, her goal was to take my life, and at that moment, these results made part of me wish that she had succeeded.

I stumbled into my bedroom. I cried for hours that afternoon. All I could see was my dream in the far distance, becoming covered by a thick haze and gradually becoming fainter in front of me. I could no longer have that dream. I could no longer strive to be that athlete. I felt like my efforts for recovery were wasted.

Mum, Dad and Jo came to visit me that afternoon. After a few hours with my family, surrounded by their love and kindness, my mind managed to settle back to what I had set my heart on, recovery. I knew I couldn't quit now, if not for me, for the people closest to me. This illness had torn the family apart for the previous 12 years. The stress, the fights, the anger, the feelings of helplessness they had experienced, the blame they'd received. It was pure torment for them, just as it had been for me. So even if I couldn't be that athlete. I had to do this so we could rebuild our lives as a family and create all those happy memories that Anna had taken away over the years. If not for me for them.

Dear Jo,

Where do I even begin?

Thank you for remaining my sister even when I abandoned you and chose Anna over you. Thank you for not letting go of my hand even when I wanted to let go of yours. Thank you for refusing to give up on me when the rest of the world did.

I am sorry for destroying so many family occasions that should have created happy memories as we were growing up. I only wish we could turn back time. You deserved those memories, but my eating disorder robbed you of them. I hope we can cherish the childhood memories we did get to make, all the mischief we got up to together, all the fun times, all the times I looked up to you and tried to copy you. My inspiration as a little girl. I am so sorry this ended when I turned 12 and we lost that relationship. I am sorry Anna ruined so many Christmases, one of your favourite times of the year. I am sorry for all the times you tried to hug me, and I pushed you away, yelling at you to leave me alone. I am sorry for all the lies and excuses I made to you. I am so sorry for the fights and arguments I caused when all you were trying to do was save me. I am sorry for stealing all of Mum and Dad's attention while they desperately tried to save me from anorexia. You are remarkably strong, holding yourself together when I tried to break you apart with Anna. Yet despite all of this. You remained there for me, every day, when I was in hospital, when I was at home and even when you flew halfway around the world to live in Australia, I knew you were there for me morning or night. Thank you for your love, compassion, and patience.

You always tried your best to lighten the mood, stop me crying, hold my hand and all these years into recovery, you are always there when I have those little moments of doubt. I don't even have to say anything, you just know. It has amazed me how you have become so wise about and observant of the illness. How you invested so much time learning about eating disorders and tried to understand why I acted the way I did. You genuinely did not want to lose your sister. Even when I didn't want to live, you wouldn't let me die.

I can't imagine how it must have felt to see your little sister fading before your eyes, being consumed by anorexia and oblivious to her own illness. Yet because of your persistence and love, I managed to navigate my way to some sort of recover journey. I can only hope that anyone else out there has someone as extraordinary, loving, and supportive as you during their recovery. Because I quite simply would not be where I am now without you. Thank you for believing my life was worth more than my eating disorder. I lost myself completely, and without your help, I would have never found my way back to this long journey home. To this day, you understand me, you understand where I am at, that I still have my struggles, and you understand that just because I look recovered doesn't mean I am. That is something so comforting for me because I know I will always have your hand to hold; you know this is a journey that I will be on for a long time, yet you accept me for where I am. Still, you continue to believe in me and all I do.

I am so proud and grateful to have you as my sister and finally have that relationship that we were robbed of for so many years.

Thank you for being my sister then, now and always. I love you.

Yours,

Jen (Betty)

Complex chronic pain

Despite receiving the news that I was existing in the skeleton of an 80-year-old, the following day it didn't seem as tragic. Maybe it was because not being able to see how bad my bone health was from the outside; I didn't really realize what the diagnosis was going to mean for me going forward. It was early and time for me to go to my first weigh in of the day. I curled over onto my side to get out of bed. As I did so, I felt the most excruciating pain in my lower back. I called out and the nurse came over with a look of concern as she saw the pain in my eyes.

"My back, something has happened to my back. It hurts so much," I replied.

She said it was likely I had slept awkwardly, after all I hadn't had a fall or done anything out of my normal daily routine to cause harm. So, she left my room and returned within a couple of minutes with some painkillers, to relieve the pain a little. Tears were streaming down my anguished face as I lay on the bed, scared to move. It was pain like I had never felt before. The remainder of that day was terrible. I couldn't move anywhere without feeling this horrendous pain spreading around my back. This was the first time I had ever experienced back pain and I started to sympathise with others who have experienced what was so excruciating. The hospital staff tried to reassure me that over the next few days, it would settle, and I would be fine. However, over the next few days it didn't settle. In fact the pain got worse and simultaneously it started to spread to different parts of my body. My feet started throbbing, and with every step, it felt like they were going to break, my knees felt like they were going to crack, and my hips were on fire with the pain. I was terrified. I had pain all over my body, something I had never experienced before, and no one could help me. I knew this was not linked to osteoporosis; after all that is a was a silent disease until something breaks. This was something else.

Over the next few weeks, things got worse, and I was becoming increasingly anxious and depressed as the days went on. The pain was also impacting my motivation to recover, and my parents were also recognising this. They made the suggestion that we should start using the free time I had been awarded to take me to doctor's appointments for scans, blood tests and anything else that may help to unpick this mysterious pain to understand what was happening. I agreed.

Over the next few weeks, I visited numerous doctors. I had blood tests, a three-hour MRI scan on my back and further scans on my knees, hips and ankles. All the while, we hoped that something was going to shed some light on this. So, we were puzzled when we returned to my consultant for her to say that everything had come back normal, and they couldn't find anything wrong with me. At this stage, I did question whether I was going mad, was I making this up? Was I really in pain, or had anorexia destroyed my brain as well as my body? No, this was real. I was in chronic pain, and I needed help.

We returned to the hospital that evening, and as Mum and Dad went to say goodbye, I fell onto my bed and burst into tears.

"I just want to give up. I can't do this anymore," I sobbed.

Mum tried to reassure me.

"Don't say that, Jen. You can do this, and we will do whatever it takes to get you better. Someone will be able to help. Right now, focus on keeping going with your recovery, and we will get to the bottom of this pain, we promise," she replied with love in her eyes.

They had to leave as it was late in the evening. I closed my eyes and went to sleep, which appeared to be the only time I couldn't feel the pain.

The days turned to weeks, and I continued to battle these pains while still trying to navigate my way through recovery. I was managing well considering the circumstances. My weight was increasing each week. Despite being in so much pain, I was able to break a smile every so often as I was getting closer and closer to being able to return home. I knew once I got home, I would have so much more time to try to work out what was wrong with my body and why I was in so much pain. But for now, I just had to manage it and try to function as best as I could.

The days in the hospital were becoming a little easier each week. I complying with all of my treatment. Communication with the staff became a lot easier, they knew I was on track with recovery and therefore spoke to me with more of a "friend" relationship rather than a "dictator" approach. I was given more freedom around my food choices and was now able to choose from a selection of breakfasts. Some days I was even allowed to prepare my own breakfast. Although I always being watched to make sure I put the correct amount of milk in my porridge, two tablespoons of peanut butter on my toast and a whole chopped banana in my porridge. In addition, I was allowed to pick from a choice of three different meals for lunch, and a few times a week I would be allowed to cook my own dinner. At snack time I had the opportunity to choose different snacks to have with my milk. Often I would opt for something like a granola bar or oatcakes with peanut butter. Sometimes, I would choose a bowl of porridge for my evening snack, having regained my love for porridge, which was one of my childhood favourites. It was so warming and comforting.

I was beginning to enjoy this process of exploring foods, even if they were foods that would still be deemed somewhat on my 'safe' list.

The day of freedom

It was the middle of August, and my dad's 60th birthday was approaching. I had been an inpatient now for 4 long months. My family had planned a big trip to Portugal, which had been our favourite holiday destination for many years. It had been doubtful for a while as to whether I would be allowed to go, as it all depended on how I responded to treatment and whether my health was stable enough to travel. I prayed every day I would be able to go with my family. I wanted to be able to have a holiday without it being spoilt for Anna, which was what had happened for so many years. Yet at the same time, I was also terrified to come out of the safety I had created in the hospital.

I remember the ward round that week so clearly. When my consultant would tell me whether I would be going on holiday with my family. I walked into my session and saw the team in front of me, their expressions bright with beaming smiles. This was different from my first ward round, where everyone looked stern, serious and disappointed in me. My consultant gave me a big grin, and firstly she asked me how I felt things were going. I was honest and said I knew I had a long way to go, but I felt I was making good progress with my recovery.

She smiled and said to me, *"Jennifer, after much consideration, as your care team, we feel that you are ready to take that step back into the world again. You have been a compliant patient; you have conformed to every rule we set, and you have consistently gained 1kg every week. We are confident that you will be able to continue your recovery as a day patient three to four days a week and spend the remaining days of the week surrounded by your loving family at home. In addition, we are happy for you to go on holiday with your family."*

When I heard those words, tears began to stream down my face, but this time not because of the pain and suffering from Anna. These were happy tears, tears of pride and joy. I was about to get a taste of life again, and I was determined to make sure Anna wasn't going to spoil this holiday.

That day that I went home was full of mixed emotions. It was so very strange, and truthfully, I felt very lost. Before being admitted to the hospital, I had deemed it the worst place in the world and couldn't see myself coping in the inpatient unit, describing it as a prison. Yet now I was being released, I felt insecure and uncertain how to navigate my way in the real world. The hospital had provided four walls that gave me a sense of comfort and protection, providing structure. A place where I could accept my identity with an eating disorder. I was unsure how to make this transition back to independence? I was not sure at that point, but I knew I would find my way. I had the support of my family, and I was determined to make it work.

The first couple of weeks at home combined with my day-patient treatment were strange and challenging. The first night back in my own bed, in my own bedroom, felt so comforting but terrifying at the same time. Despite spending every night in the hospital wanting nothing more than to be living back home, there were so many memories of Anna at home. It was scary, I had left the safety of the hospital, and it was almost harder now than during the early stages. I was also beginning to approach my target weight, which came with a lot of fear, worry and anxiety. The question nearly every anorexic who must restore weight asks is, what if I just keep gaining weight? What if I can't stop? What if people don't accept me in this new body, my athlete identity will be lost, I won't be good enough.

Looking back, I can see how exhausting every day was with the irrational thoughts about recovery. I wanted to continue, but I was so scared, so very scared. My family were incredible, doing everything they possibly could, to help me settle back into home life. They knew at that time I needed to stick to mechanical eating, eating my meals at the same times I did in hospital, keeping that routine to not provoke too much anxiety for me. If my meals were not at the exact time when I had them in the hospital I would panic, get agitated and be overwhelmed with anxiety. This is quite common for many individuals during their recovery to need to stick to regimented plans, I guess another form of control and perceived safety. It was a very difficult time to navigate my way again in the world. The inpatient ward almost led me to become institutionalized, with all these ingrained habits. I could see how obsessive I was around these routines that had been created. I feared, as well as my parents, that these habits may now stay with me forever.

Leaving the inpatient treatment also allowed for more time to unpick the unexplained pain I was still living with. I started working with a pain coach in London, Richmond Stace. This was a real breakthrough for me. Nothing else had worked, but Richmond had a profound impact on me. The trauma and emotional stress my body had gone through had quite literally placed my body into a state where it was under threat all the time. In essence I had become sensitized to pain. Fearing danger as a response, my brain would send out pain signals. The pain I was experiencing was not due to tissue damage or injury. It was my brain trying to protect me from harm. However, in reality, there was no harm. The work I did with Richmond was to teach my brain that I was safe, enable my body to leave the permanent threat it was experiencing and navigate back to balance. We worked on many mindfulness practices, breathing techniques as well as tuning in to my values. Focusing on what I want in life and not zooming in what I did not want.

It was quite incredible the impact these practices and tools had on my chronic pain, and I still use them today when I experience pain flare-ups. I also noticed patterns around my pain. When I would experience heightened stress or anxiety during recovery my pain levels would increase. This explained to me how much impact my emotions were having on my physical being. Despite the discomfort and undesirable sensations, I had to (and still do to some extent today) experience with this chronic pain condition, I feel it enabled me to gain a deeper appreciation for the mind, body connection. To truly appreciate how the body is this incredible machine that sometimes does things that we don't always understand. However, with time we realise it is always trying to work for us, not against us.

A family holiday minus Anna

Dads 60th birthday soon came round in August 2016. I had been discharged as an inpatient, but I was still being seen as a day patient three to four days a week. As a family, we were getting ourselves ready for Dad's birthday holiday, and the excitement was building. Me, well I was starting to settle in to being at home again. Although it felt so strange to sleep in my own bed and not be woken each morning to be weighed. To have more options available for meals and snacks. Mum, Dad and Jo were providing me with so much love and support to ensure I was keeping to my meal plan to make sure I achieved the further weight gain I required, to keep me on track with recovery. It was still early days. When I was feeling up to it, we also began to experiment with new recipes and new foods that I wanted to try. For a while, we were all living with a little disbelief that after so long I was now able to try eating new foods, foods I had avoided for so many years. I know my family felt such relief and were so happy that I was sat there eating 'normally'. The fact I was eating bread, that I could share a meal with them without arguments, and that I could laugh and smile and have a civilized conversation with them. I was still very regimented with my time schedules. However, still I hoped that going on holiday would help me to challenge these behaviours and break some of these patterns.

The following day, we were up very early to get the taxi to the airport to go to Portugal. It was so exciting! I couldn't quite believe that this time last week, I was an inpatient in an eating disorder unit. Now I was about to go on our first family holiday that was not going to be ruined by Anna. The flight was on time and after a short two- and a-bit hours on the plane, we arrived in Portugal. We picked up the hire car and Dad drove us to the villa where we had spent so many family holidays over the years. That afternoon some family friends, who had also flown out that day to celebrate Dad's birthday with us came round for afternoon drinks. It was just wonderful. We went out for dinner as a family that evening, without me having a panic or stressing because we were not eating at 6.00pm. This was a big accomplishment for me, on our first night of the holiday I was able to navigate eating later. I was ok.

We arrived at the restaurant and ordered our favourite meal. A meal my sister and I had grown up on with so many holidays in Portugal. We ordered a whole grilled seabass for the 4 of us with vegetables, new potatoes and salad. It was the most wonderful experience, eating this meal with my family, without being consumed by Anna. I was able to savour the flavours of the food, the connection with my family, and enjoy being in the moment. We finished the meal with a fruit platter and yummy ice cream, and again, this was such a joy to take in all the different flavours. We sat there and rather than my family and I debating whether I would eat the ice cream we were now debating which one was the tastiest. How things had changed.

The holiday continued to go well. I would be lying to say it was completely free from struggles. We did have to keep checking up to make sure that I was still eating enough and having my snacks during the day to prevent me from losing weight on. This for me was mentally quite challenging as the food in Portugal was not the same as in the UK. I couldn't have the control and safety that I felt I had in the UK. Recognising my increased anxiety my family knew I was finding this hard. They kept reminding me how well I was doing and supported me, knowing that I was showing such bravery experimenting with some new foods. I felt so lucky that I had a family who truly understood my journey. Not everyone who suffers is so lucky, but I was blessed with love around me to help me keep pushing Anna further and further away.

I knew the day of Dad's birthday itself was going to be one

of the biggest challenges for me. Dad had booked a restaurant he loved. It was a tasting restaurant which involved an eight-course meal, lots of little meals together. I knew I was going to find this difficult, and my family were keenly aware of this fact too. In the lead, up to the evening, my sister reassured me.

"It's OK, Jen, you can sit next to me, and we will work through it together, and you don't have to eat everything. You do what you feel you can, and I will be there for you all the way. No one is going to force you to have anything you don't want to tonight. Just see if you can enjoy the occasion," she said to me.

Knowing I had her support made it that little bit easier, but I was still very nervous about the event. Despite this, thankfully the evening itself wasn't as disastrous as I had imagined it might be. I managed to eat a little of each meal and tried foods I had not eaten for a very long time, including pork, red meat, and some delicious desserts. It wasn't easy, and I did feel anxious, especially afterwards, but my family and our friends were incredible. They did not draw attention to the fact they knew I would find this hard; they just treated me like everyone else, which always helps. My sister and Mum did keep looking at me with reassurance, reminding me how well I was doing. Fortunately, I managed to hold things together that night, and we had a lovely evening celebrating Dad's birthday.

The following day, I woke feeling overwhelmed with anxiety. Anna tried to creep back in, demanding I punish myself with a grueling exercise regime after the night before. At that moment, I felt I couldn't argue back with her, and I gave in by taking myself on to the balcony and doing a bodyweight exercise session. I was very well aware in this moment that I was not over anorexia yet, I had a way to go, and I was becoming more and more aware of my triggers, things that really set me off, allowing Anna to raise her voice.

I felt a little ashamed of myself for giving at to Anna in the moment, but at the same time, I also knew I needed to be kind to myself and acknowledge that the previous night was a massive achievement. The fact I completed an exercise session to compensate did demonstrate I was still battling, but I tried to focus on what I did well the night before rather than beating myself up that morning.

I also reminded myself of all the coping mechanisms I had created to help get me back on track for the rest of the day:

1) 3 meals and 3 snacks a day.

2) Acknowledge my thoughts and feelings around food are in my head.

3) Focus on the benefits of recovery over the risks.

4) Remember how Anna ruined so many years of my life.

5) Ask for help and support when I need it.

6) Challenge my eating disorder beliefs.

University goals

The holiday continued to be a wonderful break. I felt so incredibly grateful to have such a joyful experience after being denied my happiness for so many years. On the day after Dad's birthday, we were at the beach and Dad, and I decided to head for a walk along with water's edge. This was so special for me and for Dad. Being able to engage and enjoy some time alone with Dad, father and daughter bonding time was something we had lost for far too long. It was beautiful we were finally able to enjoy some quality time together.

Dad asked me, "Jen, what would you like to do when we go home? Do you want to take some time at home, to rest, to reflect and make plans for what you may like to do in the future, or do you want to do something else?"

I turned to him and replied *"Dad, I think I want to try again to get my degree. I know I have tried before and Anna got in my way, but I would like to try again. I know I can do it and I feel ready now."*

Dad looked back at me, *"Are you sure you want to go straight into this now? Are you sure you don't want to take some time to reflect and give yourself a chance to make sure you're fully ready?"*

But I was certain. *"No, Dad. I know I want to try now."*

He knew that when I said I was going to do something I meant it. I felt determined. I wanted something to focus on, I wanted to start moving forward with my future.

Dad replied, "Ok, I understand where you are coming from and if you are sure I will support you. However, I think it is important that if you want to do this, you should study at a university where you can live at home. That way you know you have the support from your family. Maybe we should take a look at universities closer to home?

I agreed with Dad that having support around me was very important right now and was happy to explore options closer to home. As we walked back along the beach to re-join Mum, Jo and friends, I began to create this vision in my mind. I had my sights set on starting a university course that September. I soon acted upon that vision and when we returned to the villa that afternoon I applied to the University of Kent. It was nice and local to home, only and 25-minute drive. I applied for their BSc in Sport and Exercise for Health. To my surprise, I was offered a place the following morning.

On our return to the UK, Dad and I took a trip to the university to visit the campus and meet my tutor if I accepted my place. I felt instantly at ease meeting Lucy; she was welcoming and understood my battles I had endured. She provided me with support from that very moment. She encouraged me to accept the offer and emphasized I would be fully supported throughout the degree program. My decision was made, I felt comfortable and confident I would be ok there. I felt that I had a connection with Lucy, and that was enough to tell me that this next stage of my journey was going to be a good one.

The remainder of the week was all about getting ready to start university. Knowing I was living at home made it much easier. I knew I could keep my meal routine, and nothing really had to change that much. I could continue with my recovery while studying for a degree at the same time. I also hoped to make some good friends, something I had lost out on for so many years. Having anorexia for as long as I had meant I had lost nearly all of my friends I made at school. There were only so many times, they would invite me out, only for me to say no, only so many times they could check I was OK, only for me to snap back at them in an aggressive and defensive way. All they had tried to do was care for me, but I'd shut them out for so many years. Anna made me believe I didn't need them. I don't blame them for giving up. After all, they didn't understand what was going on in my head, how could they? I didn't even understand most of the time.

The first day of university came round quickly and I had mixed emotions. I was very excited but nervous too. This was a whole new venture for me. A month ago I'd been sitting in hospital as an inpatient. Now here I was, one-day-a-week attending outpatient treatments and about to start my university degree. I remember parking my car in the university car park and walking to the lecture hall where we were to have our introductory lecture. I slipped in through the door and looked around, trying to decide where to sit. My eyes scanned the room, hoping someone would catch my eye as a friendly face. Looking over the rows of seats, my glance eventually fell on a girl, very pretty. She looked a little younger than me. She was sitting with another girl, and they were laughing together. I was drawn to her, it may sound strange, but I felt like something inside was telling me that there was something special about this girl and that she was going to become a good friend to me. I felt her energy connect with me across the room, and I chose in that moment to act on it.

I walked up the steps, snuck along the aisle and approached her.

"Do you mind if I sit here?" I asked, pointing to the seat next to her.

"Of course not, come and join us! My name's Molly, and this is Amelia," she replied. *"Come and join the fun. We were just laughing about how we look like the only ones in here who are study nerds with our laptops out, pencil cases at the ready and colour-coordinated folders."*

I could tell instantly that this would be a fun friendship. I enjoyed the rest of that first day, and I had such a great time getting to know Molly and Amelia. I was quite open with Molly early on about my battles with anorexia. She opened up to me about her struggles with bulimia. I think being so open early on shined a light for both of us, acknowledging that we had even more of a connection than we'd first realised. I was excited for this friendship to grow.

My experience at Kent was one that I could relive over and over again. The staff were incredible, and I had so much support around me from day one. My course was brilliant, and I really enjoyed the variety of modules. I continued to work on my recovery, however, I had noticed a slight change in my eating habits. University came with a lot of pressure, I placed a lot on myself again to achieve the high standards that I set. This would often create anxiety when I felt like I was not producing work to those unrealistic high standards. I needed to have something to help me feel in control again, suppress these emotions, and help me feel empowered again. I didn't want to fall back into my old ways. I didn't want Anna to steal my life again. I needed to find another way. So, I started to focus more on only eating foods that society would label as 'healthy' and ensured that I was exercising in the gym six days a week. This slowly became a new obsession, it crept up slowly but I was becoming increasingly addicted to exercise and *obsessively healthy eating'*. At the time, I think I was very vulnerable to diet culture in society, and it was almost being spoon-fed to me daily as it continued to become normalised. I was desperate however to feel this control again, and I was easily swayed by anything I read that seemed even slightly convincing.

Gradually, foods were being cut out of my diet again. First, I cut out sugar, then I started cutting out wholegrain forms of carbohydrate, then I cut out bread again, then dairy, then gluten. I was still eating, but it had all become obsessive. However, I did not see how this crept up on me, how disordered my relationship with food and exercise had become. I was obsessed with exercising every day, and if I couldn't, I'd become very anxious. I had created new rules that I now needed to stick to these 'healthy' foods, or it would promote considerable anxiety. I was petrified of sugar, and I started finding myself avoiding social occasions where I was not sure whether foods that were acceptable on my rules list would be available. I could see bad habits developing. However, I looked healthy, and people accepted these new behaviours, so maybe this was what recovery looked like maybe this was the new normal? I knew many other people who were doing the same as me, demonstrating similar behaviours, and they didn't appear to have an eating disorder? Or was this diet culture again sneaking up on me, normalizing disordered eating behaviours? Every other person seems to have a label, whether it is *Paleo, Keto, low carb, veganism from a place of restriction, fasting, detox, the list is endless. Yet as a society people are praised for their adherence to these dietary behaviours, without the recognition of the disordered nature of such practices. Immersed in an environment where harmful language is thrown around about food, exercise, and body image. It is no wonder so many of us in recovery from an eating disorder end up swapping one obsession for another. And this was exactly what was happening to me.*

A beautiful friendship

I was fast approaching the end of my second year at university. The time was going so fast. I was progressing well and achieving top grades for my assignments and exams. I guess this did not come as much of a surprise to my family. Notoriously being the perfectionist I was, I would always place myself under immense pressure to strive for the "best". Despite the fact I appeared to be managing my university workload, I was becoming further immersed in this new obsession I had created, essentially, I understand now this was a presentation of my eating disorder in a different way. I would get up before sun rise every day to go to the gym (no negotiations even if I felt tired or unwell), I was conforming to the 'healthy eating rules' I had created, gradually cutting more and more out of my diet that didn't meet diet cultures standards of "healthy". Nevertheless, I was maintaining my weight and appeared to look healthy from the outside, so while my family could see I was still not free from my battles with Anna, this period of time ended up with me sitting in a place which felt safe and comfortable without challenging the next stages of recovery.

I had built a beautiful friendship with Molly. We spent all our time together at university. She understood me and was always there to lift and support me, reminding me that I was good enough and how proud of myself I should be. She was always there for other people, so much so that sometimes I think she forgot to remind herself how incredible she was too. There was never a dull moment spent, with Molly and we shared countless amounts of laughter, which was so wonderful. Tragically, at the end of our second year, a shocking incident occurred, and I lost my new best friend. Molly was murdered. The world lost someone who quite literally brought nothing but sunshine into the lives around her.

Along with choosing to recover from anorexia, losing Molly was one of the hardest periods of my life. She was someone who had the warmest of hearts. She was the kindest friend I could ever have wished for. She lit up every room she entered with her beautiful personality, and I don't think there could have been a soul in the world who didn't love her. You only had to look at how many friends she had to show what a loved person she was.

Molly's death had such an impact on me. I struggled with further episodes of depression and emotional distress for the following few months, However I think this was only to be expected. Due to my history, my family, staff at university and care team were concerned this loss would trigger me to fall back with my recovery. It is not uncommon for periods of increased emotional distress, a loss of control, a tragedy, to send those in recovery into an eating disorder relapse. However, I was aware of this, and while I was still struggling with my eating disorder, I knew I did not want to fall back to that very dark place I was in during my time in hospital. I didn't want that, and more so, I knew that Molly would not want this to happen. So, I tried to remind myself every day that I needed to stay on track. Not just for me but for her too.

Graduation

Returning to university for my third year without Molly was a challenge. With the empty seat next to me, I felt like I had lost a part of me. The excitement of going to university and engaging in the laughter with Molly was no longer present. It was a difficult time, however, I continued to work my way through my last year for Molly as well as for myself. I worked hard and it all paid off. I was awarded a first-class honours degree with two additional awards for the most outstanding student award and the greatest contribution to university award.

I was elated, and my family were so proud. This was a huge achievement. But if I am being honest (and not to sound over-confident), I didn't expect anything less. I was still striving consistently to be this perfectionist, I was determined. I was a high achiever, all the traits that fit with those who suffer from eating disorders. I often think how those of us who experience eating disorders have such incredible strength, determination, dedication, and adherence to maintain such an incredibly debilitating illness. Ironically it is these same qualities and traits that we need to use to be able to recover and rediscover our true selves. Yet, it seems so hard for us to be able to apply these traits in a more positive manner rather than a destructive way.

The three years at university had presented me with so many challenges, from Molly's death to the smaller things like trying to learn to break my rigid routines to navigating my way through university whilst still trying to stay on track with my recovery. It had been an experience that continued to shape me. Graduation was a wonderful day for all the graduates, and despite it being the end of my undergraduate degree. Yet, I was not yet finished with my education. I had been offered a place at University College London (UCL) to study for a Masters degree in Eating Disorders and Clinical Nutrition. I wanted to begin to turn all those years I spent battling anorexia into something positive and now drive my energy into the research.

I was due to start this next chapter in September 2018, and it soon came around. I felt positive about taking on this next challenge and continuing to pursue my education in academia. However, what I didn't realise was that this next stage of my journey was going to reveal something more to me about myself, my eating disorder and the journey of recovery.

Questions in recovery

It was the first day of my Masters degree at UCL. It was a very different experience for me and a push out of my comfort zone. I was going from a small campus-based university to commuting into London, walking through the bustling streets to make my way to UCL which was a significantly larger university to what I was used to. I remember feeling overwhelmed by the number of people around me when I arrived. It made me feel anxious, however I tried my best to remain calm and to see if I could lean into this experience with more curiosity and excitement than fear. I arrived at the lecture theatre where I would sit my introductory session, a welcome lecture to the degree. As I entered the room it was already full of other students, most already in conversation with the person next to them. This time as I looked around, my eyes were not drawn to anyone like they had been with Molly, so I walked to the back of the room and sat myself down, and listened with intent.

The first couple of weeks did not go as well as planned. Despite my attempts at leaning into curiosity and excitement it was a fortnight of extreme anxiety, doubt, fear and tears. I was struggling with the big lifestyle change as well as being immersed in a large, busy and bustling environment. I spoke to my parents expressing my fears, my worries, but they tried to reassure me I could do this. My eating was becoming even more obsessive. My mind was becoming increasingly focused on 'health trends,' and I was constantly reading online and in books what foods I "should and shouldn't eat". I would spend hours listening to health podcasts, reading nutrition articles, and buying 'health' books on nutrition. I would walk around health food stores analysing nutritional content and ingredients, ensuring I only purchased what I considered 'pure' and 'clean'. It is terrifying how these resources, which continue to provide misinformed nutritional guidance, underpinned by diet culture are so readily available to access and essentially fuel the fire for those with eating disorders, or those at risk.

I remember the early stages of my Masters degree, I felt like I'd made a wrong decision. Everyone on the course knew so much more about nutrition, especially in the biochemistry module, where I felt hopeless. For the first time in my life, I honestly thought I wasn't clever enough to do this and felt that maybe I just needed to accept that. But at the same time, there was part of me that knew with my personality, I would feel even more a failure if I were to quit. The thing I found the hardest was the fact I was a real underdog, working my way up from the bottom of the ranks. I was not at the top of the class, and I had to learn to make peace with that. I needed to understand that it was OK not to be the best, it was good enough just to be me, to focus on my own progress and nobody else's. So, despite my fears and doubts I stuck with it and slowly but surely, I started to make progress and realise that maybe, just maybe, I was cut out for this after all. Looking back on my time at UCL, it was a year I am so grateful for, not only for the fact that I managed to obtain a distinction at the end but also for the way it helped me develop so much as a person in learning how to channel some of my destructive thoughts and emotions into more positive constructive outcomes.

In addition to my academic progress, there was something even bigger dawning in my consciousness. Despite my not wanting to acknowledge it at first, this period of time confirmed to me that I was very much living a life that can only be described as "functionally recovered". I was still very much living trapped inside an eating disorder, but in a way that was deemed acceptable in society. From the outside I appeared healthy, but inside I was living a constant battle again. This time not typically the restrictive anorexic, instead the obsessed orthorexic, whereby I would only eat foods I deemed healthy, and I would exercise obsessively every day. I started becoming aware of the nutrition habits and patterns of others around me. I aspired to have a 'fitness' body, like the ones you see in fitness magazines. I believed if I had that, I would be happy. I would be worthy.

Each week I went to university, I noticed how some of the girls on my course had experienced eating disorders previously. They were now in a place where they had reached full recovery, where they would sit down and have complete freedom over what they ate. Some days they would bring in a salad for lunch, but on other days they would have a sandwich followed by a slice of cake for a friend's birthday. I would see them go to the café at different times of the day, dependent on their hunger cues, and order what they truly wanted, without having to listen to any rules around whether it was "healthy" or not.

I remember I would gaze over at the girls who had this freedom, feeling almost envious, knowing that I was not in a place to be able to enjoy social occasions like that or to experience that flexibility around food. I longed to be able to sit down and eat food without even thinking about whether it was deemed 'healthy' or not, without thinking about the nutritional content. Just being able to be in the moment, enjoying the food and the occasion with friends. To see food as food and nothing more, nothing less. However, at the same time as noticing these girls with complete food freedom, I also began to notice others who had spoken to me about a history of an eating disorder but claimed to be recovered, yet they were demonstrating patterns around food and exercise that were similar to my own. They would never eat anything deemed 'unhealthy', they were very strict with their eating, and I could see how these behaviours mirrored mine.

I started to question where I was with my recovery and began to ask myself: do you really fit the criteria for full recovery? Do you really want to continue in this way for the rest of your life? To answer some of these questions, I decided to write down what I truly believed recovery looked like, with real integrity. Here is what I found:

1) Last-minute lunches or drinks with family or friends, having fun without feeling the slightest twinge of guilt (recovery is not: stressing about what food will be available, whether I have time to exercise, or getting anxious about the food I've eaten).

2) It is eating an extra snack during the day because I'm hungry and listening to my body rather than listening to Anna.

3) It is being able to look in the mirror and accept myself for everything I am.

4) It is exercising when I feel I want to and not when I don't feel like it. It is exercising for the right reasons and has nothing to do with changing the shape of my body or burning calories.

5) Recovery is not fearing any foods and removing a black-and-white thought process around what is healthy or unhealthy. All foods can be part of a healthy diet.

6) Recovery is living without Anna constantly speaking to me, criticizing me about my recovery.

7) Recovery is about freedom and being able to enjoy all those foods I loved as a child again.

8) Recovery is health and happiness.

9) Recovery is laughter, love, adventures, happy memories and living in the moment.

10) Recovery is life.

Writing this list helped me realise I was far from attaining a full recovery. I still had issues I needed to overcome. However, this time living in a body that from the outside looked 'healthy' (I use quotation marks as I know it wasn't healthy). Many people were oblivious to the fact that I still had an eating disorder. Only those who were extremely close to me could see. Sadly this is a misunderstanding of eating disorders within society. What most fail to appreciate is that you do not have to look ill to be sick, you can be any shape or size and still be suffering. Eating disorders are mental illnesses that can affect anyone. They do not discriminate.

I started to research around the eating disorder experience that I was currently encountering, as I didn't know whether it was 'normal' or not. Diet culture convinced me it was normal. The behaviours I was demonstrating were praised, but my innate wisdom told me that this was not normal. When you have lived with an eating disorder for as long as I had, it is hard to know yourself what is normal, whether you are recovered or not or whether you still appear to the outside world to have some disordered behaviours? It was around this time when I was asking myself these questions that I stumbled across work by Renee McGregor around orthorexia.

Orthorexia; defined by Steve Bratman in 1996 as "a fixation on righteous eating". Today it is more understood as the unhealthy focus on eating foods only deemed "healthy". Other foods that do not meet these criteria are avoided. This can progress to extremes. Some examples include avoiding anything containing sugar, anything that is considered "not natural", avoiding fruits one believes is too high in sugar, an immense fear of carbohydrates. However, it goes beyond the food, individuals with orthorexia will often become obsessed with exercise too and have very defined rules around their routine each day.

Learning about orthorexia I realised this sounded just like me. I was a recovering anorexic who was now developing orthorexia. But I was scared to reveal this to anyone because if people knew I was still struggling, it would have felt like I had failed. After all, everyone praised me for how incredible I was for what I had achieved. I thrived off this praise. How could I open up about the fact that I was still having these battles every day? I wasn't sure that I could. Maybe it was best I just carry on as I was? I wasn't even sure I believed any more that full recovery would even be possible for me after having been described as an "enduring case". I couldn't remember the last time in my life I felt like I had complete freedom… 12 years old was a long time ago. I did not feel like I had the strength or energy inside of me to venture on another battle. I almost felt comfortable staying in this place of perceived safety. However, I also knew this place of safety was failing to provide me with a fulfilling life, one where I was truly happy. Did I want to go through life trapped in this functionally recovered body, or did I want to be able to have the happy life I truly deserved? One where I could truly embrace this limited time I have on earth.

Christmas 2018

Christmas 2018 was fast approaching, and we were going to Australia to spend the holidays my sister, who had been living in Sydney for the past three years. We were all so excited to see her and to spend Christmas on the beach during an Australian summer. I was happy to be spending another Christmas abroad, but this time it was happiness knowing I would not be alone. I would be with my family. However, I was well aware that this Christmas would not be without my eating disorder. Months before we left, I had already planned how I would maintain my exercise regimes whilst we were away, I planned what I would eat, when I would eat and how I would maintain all the rigid rules I had created. This was the only wat I could enable myself to feel in control, safe and comfortable. Looking back, it makes me sad to think I had to plan this all in my head. Wasting so much precious energy, when really, I wish I could have been able to be excited for what Christmas was about. Enjoying this time with my family, enjoying creating memories, and not letting food or exercise consume me. I wish I could have just embraced spontaneity.

The flight itself was another thing which provoked significant anxiety for me. Not only did I know I would have some struggles with my chronic pain condition. Being confined in small spaces for a long time was notoriously something that would kick off my pain issues. However, I was also scared about how I would manage my food. I did not want to have to eat plane food. It didn't fit in with my "healthy" eating rules. So, before we left for the flight, I packed my own food. I was incredibly anxious about it and had to take multiple salad boxes in my bag. It was so obsessive. I know plane food isn't exactly the tastiest at best of times, but the extremes I went too way beyond "normal". Even the suggestion of buying something from one of the multiple cafes/ food stores in the airport was not something I would lean in to.

Despite the chaos I was causing already, I got through the flight and we arrived in Sydney, greeted by a huge hug with my sister.

The following day, Christmas Eve, we did a big Christmas Day shop, buying all the food and drink that we wanted for the celebrations. This involved a combination of both Australian and UK traditions, including prawns, fish, turkey, vegetables, salads and all the "trimmings" as well as many desserts. I found the shop quite anxiety provoking. I struggled when I saw very large amounts of food being purchased. This was despite knowing that I would maintain my rigid rules and not allow myself to explore and enjoy some different foods on the occasion.

On Christmas day, I woke at 5.30am to head down to a 24-hour gym to make sure I got my workout in that day. I could not miss it, not even on Christmas Day. Some people would commend me and say they are inspired by my motivation and dedication. But inside, I know this behaviour that day was driven by my eating disorder. Christmas morning never used to be a morning when I felt I had to get up to exercise. It used to be a morning when I had excitement to go and open presents with my family, the excitement of it being Christmas Day. Being able to relax and celebrate the occasion. That said, with the beautiful weather in Australia, doing some exercise on the morning of Christmas day does appeal. But for me this issue is more knowing that this should be a choice depending on how I feel rather than a rule.

After I came back from the gym, feeling ok now that I had ticked the exercise box. We all had breakfast together. My family having some eggs, smoked salmon and toast. Me, oats and fruit. After this, we made our way to the beach where we spent time swimming in the ocean and enjoying the Christmas morning in the sun.

About lunch time we walked on home to enjoy some time opening presents, having fun and games, before sitting down to Christmas dinner.

I managed to navigate the Christmas dinner ok too, well as best as I could. Although I still acknowledge that it was not without my eating disorder controlling my behaviour. I was still unable to be fully immersed in the celebrations. The voice in my head keeping me in check. I had made sure there were options that would fit within my 'healthy' eating rules. I stayed in my comfort zone, feeling safe and choosing to avoid any challenges to my disordered behaviours. I did the same for dessert. The tradition in Australia is pavlova, which my sister made for the family. I sat there and looked at the dessert with mixed emotions. My eating disorder thoughts had become so ingrained and controlling for so many years that I honestly believed that I did not want sweet things anymore. I did not even feel like I craved that dessert. But at the same time, I remembered my childhood, I adored sweet things, I devoured desserts. Yet it was my eating disorder that continued to try to convince me otherwise. So, whilst my family enjoyed the wonderful dessert and were able to share this occasion together, I just sat there with a bowl of fruit, believing that I preferred to have that instead. But really, I know this was because the pavlova didn't fit with my rules. Part of me wished I could just let down my guard and embrace the wonderful flavours, tastes and textures of the food, share the enjoyment with everyone else. Have the pavlova with my fruit. But I chose not to.

I guess my family had just come to accept this. They knew I was not fully recovered, and I think they had accepted that maybe this was where I was going to stay. Obviously, they would have loved nothing more than for me to reach full recovery, to be flexible, to be able to have the choice, and to be the Jen I used to be. But after all the arguments and battles we'd endured for so many years, it was just easier to let it go, especially now that I was eating and maintaining a weight that was a lot healthier than before. But I knew inside myself that I wasn't really able to fully embrace this occasion. I was still living a lie and trying to convince myself I was happy. Occasionally my Mum or sister would encourage me to try different foods, or suggest I take a day off from exercise, and just be more open to trying different things. I think I wished I could, but it all felt too scary to let go of this control I felt I had.

There were occasions on this trip where we did have confrontations, and rightly so. Looking back, I feel so ashamed about certain things I did on that holiday, but at the same time, I try not to blame myself. Eating disorders are complex, and the effect it was continuing to have on my actions, emotions and behaviours was significant and still affecting the relationships I could build with my family and friends.

On one occasion, my sister had booked a beautiful day out on a yacht. She had paid to hire this stunning boat for the day, lunch was included, and it was something she had really wanted to do with the family. The boat would take us out around the coast, and along the way, we could relax, drink, eat and jump off into the ocean, all the while creating happy memories and enjoying a really fun day. Most people would jump at the chance and be so excited about such a prospect. But not me. The first thing that came to mind was that I needed to exercise and couldn't be confined in such a small space where I wouldn't expend enough energy for the day. Secondly, what if there was no food that I could eat? What if the food did not fit in with my rules that I had?

I didn't know how to deal with the overwhelming anxiety that I felt. I just couldn't do it. So I made my excuses and said I wasn't going to go. I remember Jo feeling so incredibly sad that her little sister wasn't going to join the rest of the family. She knew this was driven by my eating disorder. Deep down so did I. We ended up having a massive argument, but in the end, she just accepted it. I wasn't going to go. My family set off for a fun day while I stayed back on my own. All the time I was trying to convince myself that my food and exercise routine was more fun. That I could have a fun day on my own sticking to my rigid rules. What nonsense, all of these rules I had in place were in fact leaving me feeling empty, lost, depressed and very lonely. I still feel guilty about that day, and I just hope my family know that if we were back there now, I would write that part of my story differently if I could.

I remember when they came home from the trip and were so eager to share the photos of their day with me. When I looked at the memories that they had made, I felt so much pain and upset inside. I wished I could have been part of that. But Anna quickly shut this thought down and praised me for my dedication and commitment to my rules.

This pattern repeated throughout the remainder of the holiday. New Year's Eve was the next event to riddle with my anxiety. My sister's friend had invited us to a roof top party where we would be able to watch the fireworks and celebrate the new year. Upon hearing this I instantly panicked, and my anxiety levels became unmanageable. Going to the party would mean no control over food, no way I could do my evening yoga session before bed. I would be staying up late, past the normal time I would obsessively stick too as "bed time", which would mean I wouldn't be up early enough in the morning, feeling fresh for my 6am gym workout. These rules and commitments were draining me both physically and mentally. It was exhausting. But I had to stick to them in my mind. So rather than choosing to challenge my eating disorder, I ran away from the difficult emotions I was experiencing, I suppressed them back deep in my stomach by erasing the very issue that was causing them. I decided I would not go. I decided I would stay at home; I told my family that I wanted to relax and have a quiet night on my own. I did not want to go and celebrate the new year with other people. Writing it down, its pure insanity, but this was all I knew. It was how I managed to get through each day, still needing to adhere to rules and routines to feel safe, to feel good enough, to find certainty in a world of uncertainty. Of course, I didn't want to stay home, but Anna did not want me to go and have fun. She wanted to make sure I obeyed the rules.

New Year's Eve arrived and my family left to celebrate together while I stayed at home. I cooked myself some dinner at 6pm, did my nightly yoga routine at 7pm and then sat on the sofa watching a movie for a little while before heading to bed at my normal time of 9.30pm. What a way to bring in the new year!

I remember sitting on the sofa that night, and I remember beginning to cry. I sat. Engaging in thought, and at that moment I asked myself a very important question that I had been avoiding for so long. "Jen, do you really want the rest of your life to be this way? To obey these rules for what? The body that you think will make you happy, to obey the rules that you think keep you safe. Do you want to continue to live this existence that is preventing you from living, preventing you from happiness? From having all the wonderful experiences, you could have if you could just let go, if you could just find the courage to move forward and leave this behind?" I knew I wanted freedom and could not do this to myself and my family anymore. I could not spend another New Year's Eve sitting on the sofa alone only to welcome the new year with Anna. Things needed to change; things had to change. I craved the happiness that I saw in other people, but I did not know how to break through to further challenge my eating disorder.

I needed help.

Time to challenge Anna, again

When we arrived back in the UK, I knew I needed to ask for help again. I wanted to move forward with my recovery and knew I could not do this without professional help. I just didn't feel I could break such ingrained behaviours without further support. I had opened up to my Mum and sister before we came home, telling them how I was still struggling. They both said they were proud of me and would be with me every step of the way. I think my family were just relieved if anything that I was finally ready to open up and speak about how I was still struggling. Without making excuses for all my disordered behaviours that they could see in me every day.

The next step was to find someone who could help me. I had no idea where to look? I had no idea who to reach out to. I had seen so many psychiatrists, counsellors and psychologists over the years and nothing seemed to help. I never really connected with anyone. I had worked with so many dieticians and nutritionists too, and again, they hadn't made anything any better. The doctor couldn't see a problem, and just praised me in a way, reinforced that my 'healthy' eating patterns were good. From his point of view, I just needed to eat more… but what they didn't see was me lying on the sofa on New Year's Eve on my own because I was scared to eat food that wasn't on my 'OK' list. He didn't see me go into a full- panic if I was served something with sugar as an ingredient if sauce was served up on a meal, or if my meal was served with carbohydrates. Food was not really the main problem. It was the emotional issues, the low self-worth, the need for certainty, the need to feel accepted that needed to be addressed, and no meal plan or persuasion could not do this.

The following week it was as if the universe heard my calling, and I stumbled across a podcast with Renee McGregor, which really resonated with me. Everything she spoke about hit home. Renee spoke about how eating disorders were misunderstood, explaining that you don't have to look ill to be suffering. At the very heart of an eating disorder is really nothing to do with food; the disorder is a coping mechanism.

For the past 15 years, my eating disorder helped me feel safe in a world full of uncertainties (creating safe food rules, safe food lists, safe exercise routines – everything to make me feel safe, in control). Renee spoke about how eating disorders represented a way to manage the emotional difficulties lying at our core that we do not want to address (uncertainty, loss, pain, inadequacy) or emotions that may be too overwhelming to deal with. Turning to food or exercise helps provide that safety, that sense of achievement, something that is admirable and praised by society (eating 'healthily' and exercising more). My eating disorder did just that and provided me with approval from the outside world. Helping me feel good enough (after all, who would like someone in a bigger body when society convinces us otherwise?). She explained how those of us who experience eating disorders are driven by perfectionism, a need for validation or to feel accepted. We experience significant anxiety about not knowing what comes next, not knowing how to navigate the world, or how to deal with low self-esteem. Yet the problem is no matter what coping mechanism you use (food, exercise, alcohol, smoking) to numb the difficult emotions, it is always temporary. The difficult emotions will always come back until you decide to deal with them and come out the other side.

What Renee said made so much sense, and it was the first time I could begin to untangle my mind around my eating disorder and what it was about, what purpose it was serving. She delved deeper too, explaining how you cannot fix someone with an eating disorder through food. You must change their behavior, dealing with the underlying emotional difficulties that are at the center of the problem. Yet no one had ever addressed any of these issues with me. From the age of 12, I had been living with these struggles, yet not one health professional ever spoke to me about my relationship with myself, my need for approval. It was always about my relationship with food.

Renee's podcast really challenged my thoughts and had got me thinking. Life had to be more than being trapped in this I decided I would reach out to Renee and see if we could start working together. It turned out to be the best decision I could have made. I remember our first Skype appointment. I told Renee I didn't know if she would be able to help me, explaining that I'd been stuck like this for so long that I couldn't see a way to get out. She gently replied that if I wanted it enough, together, we would get me back to being Jen, but she said I needed to want it. I really did want to give it my best shot. That was the start of our journey together.

Mum and I travelled to Bath the following week, where Renee was based, to have my first face-to-face appointment. This appointment highlighted that I was more tied up with my eating disorder than I cared to realise. I still had a dysfunctional relationship with food and exercise. I may not have looked sick anymore, but I was very definitely still struggling. I was just letting my means of control manifest in a different way, to manage the emotional struggles that I still needed to suppress. I was going to have to explore some deep and dark layers in order to move forward with my recovery. As painful as it was to hear Renee explain to me how I was still so trapped in this and how I was going to have to venture on a whole new challenge if I wanted to recover, part of me was relieved that I could finally allow myself to acknowledge this, and furthermore to not feel ashamed.

Renee didn't give me a meal plan while we worked together. We worked on my beliefs about myself and my actions, then moving on to challenge those beliefs. Renee would ask me to challenge my behaviors, setting me the task of overcoming a fear food. This seemed impossible to me, but I also knew that if I ever wanted to recover, I needed to face my fears head-on. I needed to change my habits and knew that by doing so, I'd be a step closer to recovery. So, I tried that week to see if I could challenge myself, just a little bit, but I was so stuck in my ways that I couldn't bring myself to commit. It was too overwhelming, and the anxiety would just consume me so much that I would back out every time I went to challenge

Having made this decision to go to the next step with my recovery, I also knew I needed to break my rigid routines. Living to strict time schedules every day was not helping me to find any joy in my life. Having my meals at exactly the same time every day, exercising at the same times every day, even taking a bath at the same time, going to bed at the same time, was ridiculous. However, still I couldn't change it, because it kept me feeling safe. I knew I needed to start going out, socializing. I was never going to meet new friends or, what's more, meet a partner by sticking to my same routine of gym, daily walks and yoga in my bedroom each night.

I made a decision one night that I would create a profile on a dating app, maybe this could be a start. I figured that if someone invited me on a date for dinner at 7pm, I could not tell them that I don't eat dinner at that time and refuse to go just because it wasn't 6pm. I would have to commit if I wanted to meet up. I created a profile and started being active on the app. A week later, I had my first match, and I was ready to go on my first date. I had been chatting to this guy for a while. We seemed to have lots in common and decided we would meet for a walk in Greenwich Park.

I had never been on a date from a dating app before, and I was so nervous before meeting him. As it turned out, I had a really nice time on the date, we got on well and a second date was arranged for a few days later. But more importantly, this date was a massive breakthrough for me. The first for a long time. While we were in Greenwich, he asked me if I wanted to go for a coffee. At the time, I didn't like coffee but said I would have a tea or something. We went into the coffee shop, and I analysed the menu, looking for herbal tea, as these were on my *'safe list'*. I noticed a matcha tea on the menu. I knew matcha had been claimed to have many health benefits, so I thought I would go for that. We ordered, and while he waited for the drinks, I went to get a table. As he came over with the drinks, my eyes were drawn to the green matcha tea, he was bringing me. This was not a tea as I expected. It was in fact, a matcha latte, made with creamy full-fat milk in a long, tall glass.

Anxiety immediately swallowed me up. I'm surprised he didn't notice, as my face went must have looked like I saw a ghost. He put the drink down in front of me, and my eyes were glued to the glass. I was petrified. What could I do? Here I was with a guy who I liked who had just brought me a drink. I couldn't have a battle now with Anna. I couldn't kick off. I knew there was no alternative, now was the moment that I was going to have to challenge a fear food, full-fat milk, I was going to do it.

We sat together. We talked and I slowly started to drink. I think it helped that I was with him in a relaxed environment. It took me quite a while, but I managed to finish the latte. I was riddled with anxiety, and Anna was trying hard to make me feel guilty for what I'd just done. She tried to tell me I now needed to exercise and restrict myself for the rest of the day. But I knew this would defeat the whole point and that if I were to listen to Anna, I would not be aiming for recovery.

I needed to challenge these thoughts and tried to replace them with pride and joy. Pride for having challenged myself with food that petrified me and joy for the fact that I had been able to enjoy it at the time. I was able to enjoy the experience for what it was, without Anna. I soon realised that a good way for me to challenge myself (at least in the beginning) might be to put myself in positions where I had no choice but to break my routines. To challenge my food rules and my obsessions with rigid exercise schedules.

Over the coming weeks, I took myself on many dates. None of them led to anything romantically. However, what they did lead to were personal milestones like eating Nando's for the first time in 12 years, going on my first night out dancing with friends and sleeping in until 8am the following morning, having my first alcoholic drink and having sex for the first time. All things which many people at my age do without much thought, but for me these were things I had been unable to do for so many years under the orders of Anna. It was a time where I stopped to "smell the roses" of the little joys to be found in life.

I was starting to realise that having this freedom was actually way more fun than sticking to her rules. I'm not suggesting for that I'd encourage doing all these things every day. But relaxing around routines, letting down my guard and knowing that changing things did not mean anything bad happened helped me to acknowledge that I could have balance in my life and that I had a choice. A choice to get up at 5.30am for a gym session if I wanted to, or I could choose to sleep into 8am and rest if it felt more appealing. I could choose to have chicken and chips one night because it's what I want or chooses to have a chicken salad another night because I fancy something lighter. I did not have to be dictated to by anyone. Or by what society deems the *'healthier'* option… because sometimes the healthier option may be more nuanced. For someone overcoming an eating disorder, the healthier option might be the chocolate cake over the salad, the wild night out over the quiet night in. Because health as I was starting to realise is more than just food and exercise. Mental health is just as important as physical health.

My family started noticing subtle changes in me too. Mum and Dad saw that I was out more, pleased that I was going out in the evenings rather than shutting myself in my bedroom and that I was experimenting with a few new foods. I could see how happy they were for me, that their 26-year-old daughter was starting to get her life back, the kind of life that every 26-year-old deserves to experience. This continued over the next month or two. I persisted in tiptoeing my way further forward with recovery. However, something that Renee was very concerned about was that my menstrual cycle still had not returned. I was 27 and hadn't had a menstrual cycle since the age of 12. It was not known whether I could have children, furthermore, my bone health was never going to improve unless I could get my menstrual cycle back. I was taking hormone replacement therapy to support my bones at this time. But this was always meant to be a temporary support until I restored my energy sufficiently to regain menses. I had already experienced two stress fractures because of my osteoporosis so we had not much choice but to put me on the hormone replacement therapy.

Renee encouraged me to make an effort to eat more as I was clearly still not eating quite enough to support the energy I was expending. I knew this. It's a feeling I can't explain; I knew my bone health was important to me and didn't want to have the bones of an 80-year-old (and knew what I needed to do to work on improving them). But at the same time, I couldn't seem to challenge Anna enough to break the remaining rules that she still had in place. I could not escape the belief system I had set up around myself. I found it hard living in a body that was acceptable in society yet still needed to learn to be ok with pushing myself further. My brain exhausted with constant battles, as I tried to keep tapping into "intelligence and integrity" over what my eating disorder wanted me to believe.

That evening feeling a little muddles, I decided to write a letter to my younger self and take myself back to the time I fell out of love with me, out of love with my body.

"Little Jen I you are imperfectly perfect just as you are. You

do not need to change to be accepted in this world. You do not need to be the best at everything to be loved. External validation means sweet fuck all if you cannot even validate yourself for the unique person, you are. You are so much more than a body – and in truth, your body is the least interesting thing about you. You have spent far too long hating this home, this body that has carried and nurtured you every day. You have also spent a long time trying to be best friends with this body, but maybe it is time to change this and try to be best friends with yourself – perhaps that is where you might begin to realise that you are enough just as you are."

Masters complete...

In September 2019, I had received my Masters results. To think that in my first week, I was prepared to quit, and now I was at the end of the course with a distinction. I felt very proud, as did my family. It had been a very challenging year, a year of so much growth and progress. Upon receiving these results, I began to turn my attention to what I wanted to do next. I still wasn't sure what career path I wanted to take at this point. I was approaching my 28th birthday, I felt maybe I should have a bit of a plan, or some sort of direction. I knew part-time yoga teaching was not going to fit the bill, and despite being qualified as a nutritionist with my Masters degree, I didn't feel this was the right path for someone who was still having her own struggles with an eating disorder. It just didn't feel like it was my truth. Something inside was telling me I was put on this planet for another purpose. I was just yet to understand what that was.

I sat with the unknown for a while. I questioned myself, exploring what I enjoyed and where I could see myself. I knew I thrived in education. I loved to write. Was that because I seemed to do well? Was it because I still needed that external validation of achieving top marks to show that I was good enough? Maybe, but at the same time, it was something that I enjoyed, and I thrived under pressure. I also knew I was still passionate about the area of eating disorders, and I wanted to be able to put something back into that field. My eating disorder was something that had taken so much of my life away, which I saw as such a negative period of my life. I now needed to challenge that and turn it into something that didn't destroy me but recreated me.

I decided that I would stay in the world of education and

apply for a PhD. This would enable me to remain in the world of research while focusing on eating disorders for my project. I could work on this while trying to campaign for eating disorders and mental health. I decided to throw another ingredient into this plan. It had always been my dream to move to Australia, where I truly believed the lifestyle would suit me better, being outside in nature, enjoying the sunshine and warmer climate for most of the year. However up until that point there hadn't been an opportunity for me to travel. I decided to start researching my options, researching potential supervisors in Australia who had an interest in eating disorders or athletes with disordered eating, or anything vaguely relevant. Once I had found these individuals (I ended up with around 50) I began to construct emails to them, explaining who I was, what I wanted to do and asking whether they were aware of any PhD opportunities for someone like myself. To my surprise, I heard back from nearly all of them, some with better news than others. As a result, I ended up writing a number of research proposals over the next two months. It was intense. I was researching and writing every day to make sure my applications were strong, to give me the best chance of securing an international scholarship, as I understood that these were very hard to come by in Australia.

By the middle of November, I had submitted five applications that I felt had potential. It was an anxious wait to hear back as I hadn't planned what I would do if these didn't come to anything. But thankfully they did. I received offers from New Zealand, Perth, the United States and the Gold Coast. I would have been happy with one offer, but four was surreal and I spent most of December bouncing back and forth as to which one I was going to accept. I don't think I have ever been more indecisive. But by the end of December, my decision was made. I was going to move to the Gold Coast, and I was going at the end of January. I literally gave myself one month to secure my visa, pack up my life and fly off to the other side of the world to start my PhD. It was touch and go, to say the least, with my visa arriving just two days before departure.

The emotions I experienced during this phase were quite incredible. Part of me felt extremely excited. I was finally moving to a country I had always dreamed of. I was going to be living on the Gold Coast, right on the most beautiful coastline, where the weather would be glorious most of the year. I would be researching the subject I was most passionate about, and I had the opportunity to start a brand-new chapter of my life. Yet at the same time, this was a challenging step for me, a leap of faith. Never had I lived so far from home. Never had I been away from my parents, who had showed me so much love and support throughout my life, especially during the past 16 years as I'd muddled my way through my eating disorder experiences. Part of me was incredibly nervous because they wouldn't be there to catch me every time I had a struggle, or to hug me when I felt like I couldn't do this, or chat whenever I needed it. I was also scared to leave my care team, my physio, my dietitian, my endocrinologist, my pain coach. All the people who had been part of my journey getting me to where I was today. I was going to miss the few special friends I had, who understood me and stuck by me throughout the whole journey.

But I knew this journey, this challenge was going to be worth taking. I knew it was time to leave the shoreline, explore new depths and face new adventures. It would be a big change. Change; something I had always avoided, but it had also been apparent that every time I embraced change, I took another leap forward with my recovery. I think I felt the calling this time, calling me to embrace this opportunity with more curiosity and excitement than fear.

New chapters in Australia

A few days before I was due to fly to Australia. I came across a Facebook post from the family of a girl I was in hospital with. She had passed away over Christmas due to her battles with anorexia. I lived with her in hospital, and I had spoken to her many times after leaving when she would reach out to me asking how I was and how she so desperately wanted to win her battle with anorexia. It was frightening to hear the news and also extremely saddening that a girl so young, 25 years old with her life ahead of her, was robbed by anorexia. Sadly, she is one of many. Hearing this sad news led me to think back to all the times I had been told in hospital about how I would die if I did not accept treatment to help me recover. At the time these comments appeared to be empty threats with no meaning to me. But hearing of this tragic news made it so much more real. That could have been me.

The 24th of January 2020 arrived, and it was time to say goodbye to the UK as I took that big leap of faith and moved to Australia. Hugging my parents' goodbye at the airport was a moment that I'll hold close to my heart forever. I could relive it over and over again. Mum wrapped me in her arms.

She said softly, "Darling, we love you so, so much, and we will miss you more than you can imagine. Go and chase that dream."

Both of us were sobbing, and I just stayed cuddled up in her arms, not wanting to let go. When I eventually did, Dad nestled me close to his chest, and tears began to fall down his face.

"Look after yourself. I love you," he whispered in my ear,

and with that, he gently pushed me away.

I knew that the push was to say, it's time for you to fly, time for you to go and live your life. But at the same time, it was the moment he realised that his little girl, his youngest daughter who had spent her whole life reliant on her parents' love and support was about to become independent. Obviously, the love and support would not end, but it wouldn't be a hug every day when I was struggling, or the kiss goodnight, or the physical presence of one another in the house, warming my heart. As I made my way towards security, I took one glance back, still crying but trying to remain composed. I saw Mum now nestled in Dad's arms, both of them still crying. I turned away and didn't look back again; it was time to take the next chapter and embrace it.

The flight was long however I did manage to get a few hours' sleep on the first leg down to Hong Kong before having a few hours transit. The second flight I was restless and just itching to arrive in Sydney, where I would spend a week with my sister. During that time, I spoke with her a lot about the things I had achieved back home since we were last together, and I think she noticed the change in me, the progress I was making. We had a great week together, and I got to meet her partner Billy for the first time, which was exciting. Jo and I discussed how I was feeling in myself and my recovery during this time, something we could not previously do.

I guess speaking openly about my eating disorder and my recovery to anyone, had always been something I found difficult and almost felt ashamed of. Maybe driven by the stigma attached. People often appear startled or lost for words when I mention the word anorexia. But as time moved on, I started to accept there was no need to be ashamed. It takes a strong individual to maintain an eating disorder and an even stronger individual to choose to recover from an eating disorder. I also began to start sharing my feelings instead of suppressing them. This was something I previously found so hard, maybe because for many years I lost the ability to identify how I was feeling, whether it be joy and sadness, fear and excitement. Anna had set the rules which meant I never actually listened to how I was feeling.

Life on the Gold Coast

After spending a beautiful week with Jo, I caught my flight up to the Gold Coast, where I would be living and working towards getting my PhD. The first few months on the Gold Coast were challenging. Still, I knew this was always going to be the case. I knew I had made an incredible decision to come here, I loved everything about the place, and I instantly knew this was going to be my home. This is where I want to stay, this is where I want my life to be, sometimes you just know.

However, not knowing anyone when I arrived and having few friends for the first few months did make me feel very isolated and alone. Additionally, three weeks after my arrival the Covid pandemic started and a month later I found myself in a lockdown.

I noticed some of my controlling behaviours began to creep their way back in. Not intentionally, but with increasing levels of anxiety and fear, I started finding safety, comfort and control by adopting very rigid and strict routines again. Going to the gym at the exact same time every morning, having lunch at 12.00pm exactly, afternoon yoga in the park, groceries on the way home, dinner at exactly 17.30pm, shower after dinner and then 30 minutes yoga before continuing with some more PhD work, evening snack at 20.15pm, read my book, lights out at 21.00pm. It all became a clock-watching game again, everything done by time, and I could see this unfolding before my eyes. I was still eating well, I had no desire to cut down on my intake, although it was all remaining under the "healthy food only" rules I still maintained. These obsessions with rigid routines, exercise and healthy foods began to take control. I tried not to be too hard on myself, acknowledging it was an extremely challenging and worrying time for the entire world during a worldwide pandemic. If this was how I needed to manage for now then maybe that was ok, provided I did not let it continue for too long without seeking support.

Despite the difficult time being along during COVID-19, and the associated challenges, I was making good progress with my PhD at Griffith University. My supervisors were brilliant, and the other PhD students seemed friendly, even if we were connecting virtually for the first year or so. During this time, I was also able to connect with the largest Eating Disorder Organizations in Australia, offering to share my lived experience and volunteer for them. I was honored when the Inside Out Institute for Eating Disorders invited me to share my story, to become an ambassador for them and write a blog article for their website. I was also invited to take part in a news piece for them on eating disorder recovery and how the COVID-19 pandemic had impacted this during lockdown.

Over the coming months I continued to try to embrace as best as I could this next stage of my journey. Knowing that the next couple of years were going to challenge me in so many ways with my PhD, as well as my recovery. However, I felt I was in a strong enough position to face these challenges, I was ready for change, growth and development. However, I recognised that during my first 6 months, I had buried my recovery journey under the carpet a little. I was so focused on my research, settling into a new home, trying to navigate lockdown that I forgot to pay attention to number one; myself. I was on autopilot every day, focused so much on other things that I forgot to show myself any kindness, compassion and support.

It was just after the 6-month mark in Australia where I realised the sacrifice, I was making by ignoring me, and deciding to reach out. I was getting more and more frustrated that my rigid routines were becoming normal again, but I could not seem to break them. I also knew I was very much not over the last hurdle with my recovery.

In truth, part of me questioned whether I could even jump that last hurdle. It was like being attached to an elastic band, I kept trying to pull away, putting the band under tension, but every time I tried, it just kept pulling me back. Pulling me back to that comfort zone, the pace of safety, where I felt in control. But this place of perceived safety was, in fact, what would be holding me back, a place that was preventing me from seeking complete freedom from Anna.

I knew I needed to try something new, break into the next part of my recovery journey. I didn't know how it would work, but I was prepared to give it a good shot. So, I reached out once again to Renee, asking whether she could continue working with me remotely from the UK, and she so kindly agreed. I felt anxious about this prospect, but deep down, I knew that this uncertainty consuming me was actually a sign that I needed to try to push myself even further towards recovery, because if not now, when…?

Sweet tastes of life

After spending a few months feeling like I was making little progress with my recovery, I started to think maybe this was where my recovery stopped. Maybe I won't ever reach full recovery? What does full recovery even look like? Maybe I am a chronic case who will always sit at this 75%, functionally recovered mark. Appearing healthy, fitting in with society's mold, yet still having body image issues, fears over certain foods and rigid routines. I was having online appointments with Renee back in the UK, however, I felt these were not impacting me like before? Was this a sign I was never going to reach complete freedom? I wanted to progress with my recovery but was finding it was as if I had hit a roadblock.

Despite my ongoing challenges with recovery, I was settling well into Gold Coast life. I had found a love for ocean swimming and joined the open water swimmers club here on the coast. This group became very special to me, almost like an adopted family. I was very welcome in this group. Swimming with them four times a week in the ocean proved very therapeutic and enjoyable for me. I count down the hours until it is time to swim again in the ocean, to move my body in a way that feels so free, to explore the ocean floor. I think what I found with ocean swimming, which I connect with is the idea that every day we show up. We have no idea what conditions we will face, rough, calm, big, small, yet we must commit and go with the flow. The ocean dictates how I will swim, how I will breathe. The ocean is always moving in ways I must adapt to each day. To show up and let fear be left behind for curiosity and excitement. Being immersed in the water, away from the noise of the land, finding moments of peace allowing the chaos of my mind to be silenced while I swim. For me ocean swimming is like a metaphor for life in that sense.

I also joined a Latin dance school, setting myself a new challenge to learn how to salsa and bachata. This again was something I never imagined would be part of my life journey, but I am so glad it is. Just like swimming I found I become completely present in the moment when dancing. And I never fail to leave without a smile on my face. I was putting myself out there to meet new people, try new things and find my social skills again.

In addition to building social connections with groups, I was also trying to interact socially by going out with friends for meals, coffee, walks, anything really to build these connections. One afternoon I was invited for dinner with some friends at a street food market. I agreed to go. When we arrived, I walked around checking out the stalls, instantly trying a find a stall that I considered 'safe'. Foods that would not cause anxiety, foods that fit my 'healthy' rules that I still obeyed. I appreciate, for people who may not have struggled with an eating disorder, these behaviours seem strange. Why can't we just go and pick whatever food we like? To be truthful, I think if we knew the answer to this, recovery would be so much easier. It's complex. Sometimes I do not even understand myself. But all I can find is that staying in my 'comfort zone' provided me with a sense of control, keeping everything in this neat, tidy box that I wanted, keeping everything in line with the rules Anna had set all those years ago.

I eventually found a Greek stall that served grilled chicken with a Greek salad and hummus. I ordered this as I knew it would not cause me too much anxiety. Some of my other friends picked the Italian stall and ordered pasta. I knew inside I felt envious of their spontaneity of responding to what they truly "desired" rather than picking based on any food rules. Nevertheless, we sat down together and began to eat whilst listening to the band playing. Before I knew it, one of my friends asked me if I would like to try some of his pasta. I felt panic, fear, and a knot in my stomach. How was I going to navigate this? My instant reaction in my head was to shut him down, say no, say I didn't like pasta, make up any excuse to avoid it. Pasta was not on my 'safe' list. But at the same time, I didn't want to create a fuss. I couldn't have a battle with Anna now. So, at that moment, I decided it was the time to take a step forward on recovery, now was the time to try pasta for the first time for far too long. I closed my eyes and tentatively tasted a mouthful of his pasta. I was anxious, but I was also excited. Fortunately, maybe because my friends had made me feel quite relaxed, the experience was incredible, the textures and the taste were amazing.

Despite the initial anxiety, I felt so proud of myself. For most people, a mouthful of pasta is something they do without even dedicating any thought to apart from the pleasure it provides to the taste sensations, for the satisfaction. Still, for me, this was a big step, a big recovery win. What I found most interesting though, in that moment, was how I spent sixteen years trying to overcome fears of foods, and nothing seemed to work. I could never seem to find the courage, the bravery to take that leap.

Yet, sat at that moment, I felt relaxed in the environment. Only then did this lead me to take the next step? We sat for a while after dinner before the same friend who offered me a bite of pasta stood up and said he would buy dessert for everyone. He asked me whether I wanted anything, and I declined. The mouthful of pasta was enough of a challenge for one night. But when he came back to the table, he was holding not 1, not 2 but 3 desserts in his hand. Placing them down on the table, he insisted we all share the desserts together. There was a chocolate brownie with ice cream, a tiramisu and a meringue-based dessert. My eyes were instantly drawn to the fact there were multiple spoons in his hand, one of which was given straight to me. Again, I knew inside now was not the time to create a fuss, to back down. But at the same time, I was not sure how was I going to do this? The pasta was enough of a challenge. I couldn't possibly have some dessert too. Or could I? Could

I challenge myself through two recovery wins in one night? It is only my thoughts that were going to stop me, nothing else. So, I decided at that moment, somehow, I was going to have to find the courage, the strength and bravery to eat some of these desserts.

Slowly I took a small bit of the brownie and ice cream. The emotions were like a roller coaster. Part of me felt petrified and anxious, but the other part felt incredibly proud and reminded after so many years that desserts taste incredible. The sweetness, the contrasting textures, the yumminess. From dinner, we had a spontaneous trip to an arcade where we played all those fun games you did as a child at the games arcade. We laughed, joked, and had the best time. I lost all concept of time. For the rest of that evening, I genuinely felt like me, experiencing the moment for what it was without any plaguing thoughts ruining my evening. I was living, having fun, experiencing a glimpse of freedom. I realised that this tasted way better than anything my eating disorder could ever bring me.

The next few weeks consisted of many more fun times over the Christmas period. Notoriously a time which can be extremely challenging for those in recovery from an eating disorder. With lots of food around, changes to routines, can provoke significant anxiety and discomfort. I was spending Christmas away from family this year, mostly due to the effects of COVID-19. This made me sad to not be able to spend it with them. However, an international Christmas with some friends turned out to be quite fun. There was a beautiful spread of foods, salads, prawns, Spanish tortillas, chicken, duck, vegetables, rice. Followed by tiramisu, cheesecake, and panettone. I tried a little of everything, which was probably the most adventurous. I have been with foods over Christmas for as long as I can remember. I knew I just had to commit, do it and know that the experience and memories made would be so much better than choosing to avoid and stick to my *'safety zone'*. It was amazing.

Despite being away from my family, Christmas memories were made, fun days out, games, laughter and dancing, it was beautiful. Yet what I found most incredible during this time was how I had managed to challenge my behaviours every day. Behaviours I had struggled to change for so long. Behaviours countless therapists had worked with me to try and overcome, behaviours I had almost given up on trying to change. Trying desserts, even if it was just a couple of mouthfuls, was huge progress for me. Foods I had once loved as a child passed my lips for the first time without Anna consuming me. I started to get a real sense that I was finally moving forward. I was finally starting to make progress to truly come back to myself, the adventurous, precocious, cheeky Jen everyone once knew. Life never tasted so sweet.

A couple of months passed, and I continued to have fun with friends. I was also still tentatively taking myself on dates. However, I did begin to question whether I truly I wanted to start a relationship with someone at this time. I think I began to realise maybe I was seeking someone to be in my life for the wrong reasons. I think it was a realization that I had been spending a lot of time wishing for someone to love me, to continue to help me feel good enough for this world. Almost as if sacrificing parts of myself, rearranging, and molding myself to ways I believed someone would love me. But I think I started to learn that in fact I had been good enough all along as I was, I had been likeable and loveable. Maybe I just needed to stay in love with me for a bit longer before letting anyone else come in.

So that was what I decided to do and the next couple of weeks I began to question myself again on what I truly felt I wanted moving forwards. I wanted to be in a place where I could be me, completely free, my authentic, messy self. With that, anyone who would come into my life would love and accept me for who I am, without me feeling I needed to be anything different. Maybe, just maybe, I needed to work on loving myself for a bit and know that even if no one else in this world loved, if I were to spend my life on my own, the love I have for myself would still be enough. I began to learn that being perfectly imperfect was what made me beautiful, and I get to be the one who validates my being in this world. I began to learn I was not put on this earth to be small, hide, shrink, or shape myself based on others' expectations or ideals. Not here to clip my wings or sit in silence or disappointment every time I stumble or fall. Born into this world to be bold, brave, and experience all of my light and dark. To let beauty ripple through me along with the pain, the magic, and the love. I, you, we are here to let life surprise us, move us, excite us, and sometimes scare us. I realised I wanted to start falling in love with all of me and all I bring to this world. Because it would be a sad life to not fall in love with the one you have no choice but to spend the rest of your life with.

Dear little Jen,

Born into this world perfect just as you were. Starting from a single cell and magically growing into this incredible gift, the vessel that contains all of you, your one and only home, your body. Growing into the complete, messy, perfectly imperfect you. But somewhere along the way, your innocence got lost. Your belief that you were good enough became a distant memory. Somewhere along the way, you looked down at this incredible home of yours with disappointment, believing it represented your worth. But your worth is so much more than your body, your achievements, successes. Your worth resides within. People love you for being uniquely you, and that is all you ever need to be.

Darling girl, you could never have controlled what happened to you when you were 12. It was not your fault that for years you battled your demons, consumed by the beast in your mind and starved from life, living your teenage years in darkness. But this story that you lived brought you to this very moment. The story may not have been the one you once wished for, but it is yours, so you must own every bit of it with pride. Embrace your journey and know that your struggles have become your greatest strengths. Please trust in years to come, you will look back on your story and understand why you needed to experience all you did. So, to my 12-year-old self, thank you for holding on for all those years, and I hope I have done you proud. Be proud of the way you fought to save yourself, be proud of every single step of your journey. Be proud of the courageous, strong lady you have become by choosing recovery. I promise I will always strive for complete freedom, just like when I was 11 again, a time when I felt good enough being me.

Love,

Older Jen

Ocean swimming, roadblocks and baby news

The next few months required a lot of hard work on my PhD, I was doing well. Although the pressure of my workload increasing and missing having my family around meant I began to take hold of some more rigid routines again. I was able to recognise these and sometimes even challenge them. I was also recognising such gratitude for the little things each day that I lost in the deepest darkest days of anorexia. One of those being connection. Connection with friends and family. Joining the open water swimming club when I moved here had turned out to be a significant part of my life, with the members of the group almost becoming like my adopted family. I never thought ocean swimming would become a passion of mine, yet I now see it as my daily "medication". There is something so special about being immersed in the sea of blue, away from the noise finding moments of peace. The chaos of my mind is silenced while I enter a state of mindfulness focusing on my breath, 1,2,3 breath, 1,2,3 breath. Ocean swimming has become a therapy for me, a cheap one at that too. The real magic though is being surrounded by those people who care, love, and understand me. That is something really special.

Belonging to such a close family, we were all feeling empty having not seen each other for so long due to the Covid pandemic. However, among the messiness of the world my sister had some exciting family news. She announced she and Billy (her partner) were expecting their first child, due in December 2021. This was wonderful news, and I was incredibly excited to be an Aunty and my parents were also elated to be expecting their first grandchild. I also found this quite an emotional time. I had the pivotal realization of how as fast life was going. The next generation of our family would be starting. Yet I still felt like we were the children of the family. A strange feeling.

Knowing that we had a little new member of the family on the way, I wanted to make sure as an Aunty I was going to be in a healthy, strong position to be the best Aunty I could be. I knew my sister and Billy would be such amazing parents, and I was thrilled for them. I wanted to make sure I could also fill these shoes of being a great Aunty.

While I continued to be excited for them on this fantastic news, it also reminded me how my battle an eating disorder really had consumed so much of my existence. Sometimes from the outside I find it hard to truly accept this was "my story". First diagnosed when my sister and I were in our youth, myself being just 12 years of age. Soon I would be reaching a milestone birthday; 30 years old. While each day I was learning more about myself, finding a new sense of freedom in some areas of my life, I knew recovery was still very much an ongoing journey, and maybe it always would be. I didn't want to live a life obsessed with my body, obsessed with the way I look. I want to be a woman who does not care what others think, who loves herself for everything she is and for everything she is not, who shows herself unconditional love every day and can embrace complete freedom from Anna. I want to be a Mum one day who goes to a café with her children and eats cake with them, laughing, enjoying the moments. I want to go on holidays and eat multiple ice creams on the beach, to enjoy all the foods on offer to me. Yet, I knew this still felt so far away.

Family reunion, Charlie's Christmas 2021

It was nearing Christmas 2021. I was missing my family; they were missing me. There had been some big milestones reached during the last two years, which we would have loved to celebrate together, mums 60th and my 30th. Yet here we were, still uncertain of when we would get to be reunited again. However, at the end of October we had some fantastic news. My parents were granted visas to travel to Australia to visit my sister in Sydney, in time for Christmas 2021 and to meet their first grandchild. This was the best news we had for the last two years and as a family we were so relieved and excited at the prospect of being together again. Mum booked her flight to arrive at the end of November, and Dad would arrive in Sydney later in December as he had to stay back in the UK for work. I was also planning to fly down to be with them for Christmas.

Baby made us wait for a good while. A week overdue before Jo endured quite a distressing labor for both her and baby. However, at 12.35am on the 11$^{th\ of}$ December 2021 we welcomed Charles (Charlie) David William Dent to the world. He was just perfect. Jo and Billy were over the moon with their little miracle, and I was instantly in love with Charlie from all the photos I received and could not wait to meet my little nephew at Christmas.

Another reason to choose recovery; to be part of my little nephew's journey, to love him and be the best aunty I can possibly be.

Dear Charlie,

You are finally here. You made it into this beautiful yet challenging world. Welcome to our crazy, loving family. I am your Aunty Jen – and you do not know it yet, but I am going to be your fun Aunty, who will do all those crazy things that no one else will agree to do with you. I will want to take you on adventures, swim in the ocean with you, play silly games, laugh at silly jokes we play, and sing with you to Disney songs (ok, I appreciate my time is limited with you on that last one). I promise I will love you completely, cheer you up when you are down and protect you as much as I can.

You are only a few days old, and you have reminded me of the purity and innocence that still exists in this world. As I write this, yes little buddy you have everyone wrapped round your little fingers already; go you little champion. I know right now your life is a blank slate, but your book is about to begin. Those crisp, clean pages are going to be filled with laughter, tears, joy, triumphs and challenges. Ohhhh and so much love, love will surround all of you. There is so much anticipation for the chapters that lay ahead for you and the magical adventures that await.

Your mummy and daddy love you more than anything in the world. And I know that they will provide you with the most wonderful upbringing and everything you need for the best life possible. Make sure you tell them you love them too; they want to hear it every now and again. Especially your mummy, she will never get bored of hearing you tell her you love her. I promise, as you grow, I will always be there for you on the brighter days as well as those that are a little dark. When mummy is shouting from the sidelines embarrassing you at your sports day, I will be there too and make it worse. When you need someone to confide in, I will listen with open ears (your aunty has had her fair share of challenges leaving her pretty equipped to help you over some of the mountains you might come up against). And when mum and dad are on your case about tidying your room, I shall remind them that they were teenagers once too.

I will always encourage you to chase down your dreams, put no limitations on what you can achieve and to always show up as yourself, no matter what. And when I say dream, dream big baby Charlie. Never believe that you are anything less than amazing and promise me you will never wish to be anyone else but you. Be kind and then a little kinder. Be generous and then show more generosity. Be the sunshine to someone's rainy day. Be brave little one, be strong and be free. This world can be hard sometimes, but always remember love and hope will get you through anything.

But here is the deal little one. You must not grow up too fast. Because this world is not ready for the great impact you are going to have. So, stay small for now, let us all fight over who gets the next cuddles with you. Do not be too quick to sit up, start crawling, walking and talking.

Baby Charlie, you are the littlest one who has ever stolen my heart, go in to the world and let you little light shine. You are loved now and always will be

From your favorite, Aunty Jen Jen x x x

A pause, for now!

Despite the years that I lost to Anna, I am finally beginning to accept my story and to see my scars as a detailed map of a courageous story. I understand that I could never have controlled what happened to me when I was 12 years old. It was never my fault that I battled my demons for years, was consumed by my mind, and starved of life by anorexia, living my teenage years in darkness. I understand now that I had to live and experience this bumpy journey to bring me to where I am today. It may not have been the journey I'd wished for, but it is mine, and I am learning to embrace it, understanding how my struggles have become my strengths.

The journey to recovery is not linear. I am forever discovering more twists, turns and roadblocks. In a way, it has become an exciting ride. Because I realise life doesn't start when I am finished. Where does "finish" even sit. I can't wait to be at that place wherever it is to enjoy the little things along the way in this journey. Some days are harder than others and if I speak with true integrity and be a realist, whilst I dream of freedom from my eating disorder entirely, I know this is something which will be ongoing for me, so for that I hold on to patience and complete trust in my journey. Anorexia has consumed my life for all my youth and young adult years. Reverse engineering all the learnt behaviours and beliefs takes time. So, while I want what is termed "full recovery", if I do fall short, I know I can still lead a meaningful and joyful life surrounded by those who love and accept me for all that I am. And this is not me being pessimistic about the prospect of achieving this goal, it is being a realist in my mind.

I am learning to trust that in years to come I will look back and I will understand my story, even if I can't completely

right now. Being 30 years old, I sometimes feel like I am lagging behind with life.
Not married, no babies, don't understanding taxes and I still find it hard to make my bed like my Mum did.

But here is the thing, I probably know myself better than I ever have done before because of my rollercoaster of a ride. I thrive my success in doing a good job at life by the countless times I have gotten back up after being knocked down, holding on to my scars with vulnerability, the loving relationships I have with family and friends, the adventures and life experiences I desire and the fact I am here today to share my story.

I want to say to my 12-year-old self, thank you for holding on through those battles you fought, thank you for not giving up when all hope was lost. I hope I have done you proud. I promise I will keep on working towards freedom in recovery like the kind of freedom I felt when I was 11 years old, a time when I felt good enough just being me. I understand that saving myself was the bravest and most courageous thing I have ever done.

I hope that if you are struggling from anorexia and have reached the end of this book, maybe I have been able to inspire and provide some hope to you that recovery is possible. Recovery is a decision you must make. It won't happen for you. It is a battle you must choose to fight, every single day. It is exhausting, but please know that life is something that you deserve. If you can find the courage and the bravery to take those steps to recovery. Despite the fear, anxiety and uncertainty that you will feel, you will get ever closer to being able to live your dreams, make them a reality. This is what life could be like under your terms, not Anna's. Never give up, I haven't, and neither should you.

For anyone who ever had a dream!

Thank you, Anna

Dear Anna,

For years I thought you were my best friend. You were always there for me when I felt like I wasn't good enough for this world. Because of you, I was able to suppress emotions that I could not face. You helped me feel safe in times of desperation. Yes, we argued a lot, but there was always something stopping me from letting you go. Maybe I needed you at that stage of my life. So, in a way I guess I will say thank you?

I now understand you were never actually my best friend; you were a brutal dictator who dominated me. You stole my freedom, my happiness, my life. I existed for so many years, brainwashed by your vicious, warped way of thinking. You made me lie to the people I love, isolate myself from the world, and left me with only you for comfort. You ruined endless opportunities. I never wanted to die, though you made me not want to live. But now I realise letting you go is something I must do.

You joined me at age 12, robbing me of my ignorance to freedom, the innocence I had in this world. Stealing my adolescent years and still today, you sometimes haunt me a. You landed me in hospital, a time when I should have been out having fun, living my best life. You made me hate me, you made me believe I was not worthy of this life, you hid and kept secrets from me, and you left me starving, tired and out of control. You made me hit lows I never thought possible and drowned me under your reign into moments where I felt my life was not worth living. You consumed me; you consumed my identity. I spent years under your control dying, when I should have been emerging into the beauty of life. But you are not my identity, I am more than you, and my life is better now as I managed to find joy in things without you. I have pushed you further away from my life, and every day, I continue try to find little pockets of "Jen" in all different places. I am far from being completely rid of you, but you will never be able to creep back in like you have done before.

I want to be able to eat vegetables and cake on the same day. I want to be free to choose to go to bed at 9pm if I'm tired or be happy to come late after dancing the night away with friends. I want to go out for dinner and choose what I actually want off the menu, not what conforms to your rules. I want to let someone love me without worrying whether my body is good enough for them. I want to love myself for being me, irrespective of what my body looks like. Because my body is not the enemy, it never was and never will be, but you made me believe it to be. This vehicle of mine is not there for destruction. It is my home, my source of strength, the place where my soul resides My body is no longer going to be my battleground. It has taken endless abuse over the years. Now it is time that my body receives all the love it deserves.

I choose life, because it is so short, fleeting and precious. I do not want to waste any more of my journey with you. I am building my walls back up, becoming that wild, ambitious, and gentle person I used to be. I am becoming this unique combination of what my history has made me and what my hopes and dreams will help me become. You robbed me of my first dream, a career as a professional athlete – how cruel of you to steal that from me. But as much as I hate you, I want to end this letter by thanking you. Because despite how dark you made those years of my life – the pain, the suffering – without you. Without this experience, I would not have been fortunate enough to become the strong, courageous individual I am today. Anna, I am not grateful for you, but I am grateful for who I have become because of you.

This is a letter to say goodbye, though I know it won't be easy to cut you off just like that.

I am sure you will still continue to haunt, and at times I will fall, but I will always get back up again. I realise I have everything I need to live this life without you taking up the space I deserve.

Goodbye Anna,

Jen

To the reader who may be supporting a loved one

Maybe right now, you are supporting a loved one. Maybe they are trapped in their illness, and you can't understand why they won't accept your help. Maybe you have been pushed away, hurt by someone you love, who is disappearing before your eyes, walking closer to death each day, yet cannot acknowledge their illness.

Please promise to not give up on this person. Do not stop loving them, do not stop speaking to them, do not stop trying. Fight with them, fight for them, fight through this darkness. Your love, care and support is needed, and one day, there will be a breakthrough, a glimmer of hope, a spark of light, and you will find that loved person somewhere deep down inside.

This may take years to find them. It may feel like you have lost that loved one forever but keep going because it will be worth it. It will be worth the battle when you reach the day that you can see your loved one smile again, without an eating disorder controlling their life, to see them laugh and reclaim the life they had before. To reach that day when you can look back on the nightmare and say, 'I am so thankful I didn't give up on you because life with you is too precious'.

Those in recovery need your continued guidance, love, encouragement, and persistence to fuel their recovery journey. They cannot do it without you, please remember that. You can be part of the solution.

If...

If you can keep your head, when all round you pasta is replaced with zucchini.

If you can trust yourself when the medical system describes you a "hopeless case", despite your strength and bravery to get this far.

If you can wait and not get tired of waiting for Instagram to ban all filters a promotion of DE.

If you can bear to listen to women tear their bodies down yet refuse to speak in this way to your beautiful home.

If you can dream of a life when pizza is not bad and broccoli is not good, they just are.

And your thoughts are immersed in the moment and not riddled with self-hatred because your tummy isn't flat.

If you can bear to hear your truth, be spoken, trapped in an illness that stole your happiness.

Yet still choose to rise, broken and bruised.

If you can make a heap of all your winnings and spend it on adventures rather than "health foods" (ironically those that promote disordered eating).

If you can commit to a destination of food freedom and body neutrality.

Where lasagne is a tasteful meal, not a list of ingredients diet culture made you fear.

If you can sit, relax, and not be consumed with the idea that you are being lazy.

If you can share your truth with the world and not feel ashamed.

If you can let them judge you yet remain unapologetically you.

If you can learn to be ok in a bigger body, one that wobbles and dimples and doesn't have to be sculpted or shaped into an ornament to be judged or admired.

And learn to know your worth is for being you.

Then yours is the earth and everything that's in it.

And which is more, you'll be a recovery warrior.

Farewell!

This isn't goodbye. I am sure we will meet again.

Yet next time you creep up, it will be through a different lens.

I remember the first day, in my mind you came,

I didn't know exactly who you were, but I decided to give you a name.

Anna, my best friend, the voice that saved my life?

Anna, my best friend, the voice that took my life.

The pain and suffering you cause me; how could I want you to stay?

Yet, without you, I was not enough. I was afraid, I decided to obey.

You ordered me, starved me, punished me, breaking me apart,

Lying in a hospital bed, fighting to stop you devouring my heart.

In a way, you helped me succeed, you helped me dominate,

Because after all, the winner for Anna is the fastest to deteriorate.

Yet you destroyed my happiness, my love, my playful adventure,

Consuming my body and mind to the point of surrender.

It is hard to say goodbye, because part of me does not want you to go,

And it's harder still because who am I without you remaining in my bio.

But maybe I can learn that life is worth more than obeying you,

Because I want freedom, adventures and all the good stuff too.

One day I want to be a mother and have cake with my little girl

Savouring the sweetness, the texture and licking the icing swirls.

And if I am to be blessed in having a son,

I want to tell him the story of a warrior and how she won.

I realise Anna, you will probably share my journey for years to come,

But the difference now is these years won't be lived so numb.

So, I guess, maybe, for now, you remain part of my show,

However, when I am brave enough to ask you to go, I need you to follow.

Because this is a goodbye, I want to be myself to rediscover the free spirit Jen,

And this time being able to shine my light through a

different lens again.

Printed in Great Britain
by Amazon